THE ONE
THAT GOT AWAY

or tales of days
when fish triumphed over anglers

Wood engravings by Christopher Wormell

MERLIN
UNWIN
·BOOKS·

First published in Great Britain by Merlin Unwin Books, 1991
Reprinted 2015

Copyright © Merlin Unwin Books, 1991

All enquiries should be addressed to:
Merlin Unwin Books Ltd
Palmers House, 7 Corve Street
Ludlow, Shropshire SY8 1DB, U.K.
www.merlinunwin.co.uk

The authors assert their moral rights to be identified with this work.
A CIP record of this book is available from the British Library.

ISBN 978-1-910723-02-9

Designed by Kingfisher Design

Printed and bound by CPI Antony Rowe Ltd, Wiltshire

CONTENTS

The Contributors   v

Publisher's Note   x

THE BASS AT THE MERE Nigel Haywood   1

LAST CAST ON DAL HARRALD Max Hastings   11

TOO SOON AN AGE Brian Clarke   21

THE FISH BY THE THISTLE Sidney Vines   29

WHEN ALL THE WORLD WAS YOUNG David Street   37

MISADVENTURE AT MALINDI Julian Paget   47

JILTED BY THE QUEEN Chris Yates   53

ISLAMORADA Neil Patterson   63

NEVER TRUST A POACHER David Steel   75

PUTTING YOURSELF ON THE LINE David Profumo   75

POOL OF THE SUMMER SHEILING Bruce Sandison   81

THE TROUT THAT SAID THANK YOU Conrad Voss Bark   91

OVER THE VOLCANO Bernard Venables   105

GOING FOR BUST Chips Keswick   117

PLAYING THE APRIL FOOL George Melly   123

ONE THAT SHOULD HAVE GOT AWAY Jeremy Paxman   131

THE MONSTER OF CLAPHAM BECK Laurence Catlow   139

THE CONTRIBUTORS

GEORGE MELLY

Professional jazz singer; music, art and film critic; author of several books – George Melly was a man of many artistic talents. He had a lifelong passion for angling, and in later life made his home in the Welsh Marches fishing on his local river, the Usk.

DAVID STEEL

The Right Honorable Lord Steel of Aikwood, was Member of Parliament for Tweedale, Ettrick and Lauderdale (1965-1983) and was leader of the Liberal Party between 1976 and 1988. He likes best to fish the rivers and lochs in or near his former Scottish border constituency.

JEREMY PAXMAN

Well-known for his tough line in interviewing on BBC's *Newsnight* (which he presented for 25 years) Jeremy Paxman also writes for national newspapers and magazines, and has written many books on subjects ranging from the British establishment, *Friends in High Places* (1991), to his portrait of a people and a nation, *The English* (1999). He currently presents the BBC programme *University Challenge*.

SIDNEY VINES

Serving with the Royal Artillery in 1944 Major Sidney Vines was among the first to land on the Normandy beaches. After the War he became a restaurateur in Southampton. He was a friend of Frank Saywer and facilitated the re-issue of Sawyer's classic *Keeper of the Stream*, followed in 1884 by a full biography of Sawyer, *Man of the Riverside*. His final book was *The English Chalk Stream*.

MAX HASTINGS

Sir Max Hastings Hastings was the first journalist to enter the liberated Port Stanley during the 1982 Falklands War. For ten years he was editor and then editor-in-chief of the *Daily Telegraph*. As a child, he preferred shooting to fishing with his father, the well-known country writer Macdonald Hastings. But in recent years, he has become a devoted salmon fisher, above all in the north of Scotland.

JULIAN PAGET

Sir Julian Paget served for twenty seven years in the Coldstream Guards retiring as a Lieutenant Colonel. He has written many books, mainly on military history, and organises battlefield tours. He is a former President of the Flyfishers' Club, London.

DAVID PROFUMO

Sea Music (1988), was David Profumo's widely-acclaimed first novel. A mad-keen angler from as early as he can remember, he now writes on fishing for various publications and is a regular contributor to *Country Life*. He co-wrote *The Magic Wheel* (1986), an anthology of fishing literature.

CHRIS YATES

Author of *The Secret Carp* and *Falling in Again*, Chris Yates has a reputation as the most articulate voice in coarse fishing. He is a professional photographer, former holder of the British rod-caught carp record (51½ lbs) and he co-presented a major TV fishing series, *A Passion for Angling*, which set the standard for the next three decades.

NIGEL HAYWOOD

Recently retired Governor of the Falkland Islands, former First Secretary in the Foreign Office, ambassador to Estonia and Consul-General in Basra, Nigel Haywood has fished all his life.

NEIL PATTERSON

Former Creative Director of Young & Rubicam, Neil Patterson went on to co-found and run a major advertising agency. He is an ardent, globe-trotting flyfisher and fishing writer and his brilliant trout fly inventions – such as the Funneldun – have become standard chalkstream patterns.

DAVID STREET

Fishing in Wild Places (1989), an angling memoir, established Reverend Street as an exceptionally good fishing writer. He has contributed to *Trout & Salmon*, *Trout Fisherman*, *Shooting Times*, and other journals. On retirement from the priesthood, he lived in county Durham where he wrote, visited prisons... and fished.

BERNARD VENABLES

Bernard Venables, the artist and writer, is known to anglers throughout the world for his cartoon character Mr Crabtree whom he invented while working on the *Daily Mirror*. In 1953 he co-founded and directed *Angling Times* and later was founder-editor of *Creel*. His TV and radio broadcasting and his many books made him an all-round angler of Waltonian stature.

CHIPS KESWICK

Sir John 'Chips' Keswick has been a keen fisherman from the age of six when he learnt to catch small trout from Scottish burns. Nowadays, his fishing is mainly on the Test or the odd week in the Highlands. A career banker for over 50 years, he is a former Chairman of Hambros, and he is Chairman of Arsenal Football Club.

CONRAD VOSS BARK

Besides being the first man to read the news on British television, journalist Conrad Voss Bark had a distinguished career as the BBC's Parliamentary Correspondent. He wrote many novels and fishing books, including *A History of Flyfishing* and *The Dry Fly*. His wife Anne Voss Bark ran the Arundell Arms Hotel at Lifton.

BRIAN CLARKE

Author of two enduring books on trout fishing, *The Pursuit of Stillwater Trout* (1975) and *The Trout and the Fly* (1980, co-author John Goddard), Brian Clarke is the thinking angler's writer. After many years in industry he left to devote his time to writing and is Angling Correspondent for *The Times* and the *Sunday Times*.

CONTRIBUTORS

BRUCE SANDISON

Trout Lochs of Scotland (1983), the first of Bruce Sandison's books, established his credentials as one of Scotland's most well-informed anglers at the time. A prolific journalist on subjects as varied as hillwalking and local history, he became an ardent campaigner against the afforestation and peat extraction in the Flow Country, his home.

LAURENCE CATLOW

Until his recent retirement, Laurence Catlow was Head of Classics at Sedbergh School in Cumbria. He writes regularly about shooting and fishing, two of his three great passions, in various magazines including *Trout & Salmon* and *Shooting Times*. His first book, *Confessions of a Shooting Fishing Man* (1998), tackled the burning fieldsports issues of our time, including the hunting ban. He has since written *Once a Flyfisher* (2001), *Private Thoughts from a Small Shoot* (2003) and *That Strange Alchemy* (2008).

Publisher's Note

The angling press is full of photographs of anglers holding up, trophy-like, the fish they have caught. But in my view, the image most deeply engraved on every angler's heart is of a fish which never actually made it to the net: the one that got away.

This strange phenomenon distinguishes the fisherman from his sporting counterparts. Golfers, for example, tend not to speak about crucial holes they have missed; footballers would rather forget the goals they have fluffed; and pheasant shooters, perhaps closer relations, are usually embarrassed and reticent about the easy birds they have pricked but not downed. These are the low points in the sporting day, the failures, the moments to be erased from the mind.

The angler, on the other hand, dwells on the mystery of the fish he *might* have caught. Sometimes, when a particularly memorable specimen gets away, he will be moved to tell the story of it. Non-anglers might regard such accounts as wild exaggerations (and perhaps there is a tendency for anglers to endow lost fish with leviathan proportions) but these episodes are nevertheless the ones that stick in the mind, that become the stuff of dreams, that are ultimately more vivid and real than memories of anything conquered.

Hence this book: a tribute not only to the cunning, courage and spirit of fish that escaped but also to the soul of the angler, that curious fellow who can be enriched by his loss.

I hope these pages are more than just a catalogue of piscatorial defeats. The true tales you will find here come from accomplished, sometimes famous, anglers and the message they convey is one with which every fisher will identify.

Merlin Unwin

CHAPTER ONE

THE BASS AT THE MERE

Nigel Haywood

It is curious how, when we were very much younger, so many events which would have lasting consequences for our lives could tumble together into the space of a few short weeks. I can now go for months, even years, without as much happening to me as it did in the average fortnight when I was in my late teens or early twenties. Take the summer of 1977, for example.

A boiling hot day in June found me cycling from Oxford to my brother's house in Sussex. Breaking for lunch, or at least a pint or two of beer, at Henley, I was feeling rather pleased with myself. I had just finished my final examinations at the university and had, I thought, done reasonably well. If I got a First, I would go back in the autumn and take up the research place I had been offered. True, it was by no means in the bag: a *viva voce* exam in a week's time would decide. But in the meantime, there was the trip to Sussex, with the prospect, a few days later, of a weekend with a St. Anne's girl who had, over the preceding term, provided my main distraction from the intricacies of mediaeval literature. All in all, I mused over the second, rather less hurried pint, life was pretty good. And Sussex? Well, in Sussex I was going to go bass fishing.

It was not just the St. Anne's girl that had diverted my attention during the summer term. There had been the letters from my brother. He had discovered bass fishing on the Sussex coast. With the zeal of the new convert he enthused over each successive capture, and after a short while I grew fed up with reading about big fish from marks I had never seen. Before long, thoughts of Cow Gap, the Dragon's Teeth and the Mere caught me unawares as, suffering with hay-fever about as far from the sea as it was possible to get in England, I gazed out of the windows of the stuffy library, unable to do anything about them. But now, as I got back onto the bicycle, I knew that this was all about to be put right. The omens were good. It was Silver Jubilee year; that very afternoon a British player was in the process of winning the Ladies' Singles title at Wimbledon; the sun was shining and the road to Sussex beckoned.

The next morning was calm and warm. I watched the sun climb over the horizon from the reefs at the foot of Beachy Head, now exposed by a low spring tide. I was being introduced to the back-breaking job of searching under boulders for crabs to use as bait. I had never seen so many crabs before in my life. But, unfortunately, you cannot expect to catch bass on any old crab. The only ones that are any use are those which are just about to slough the shells they have outgrown. You kill the creature by jabbing a sharp knife between its eyes, peel away the shell, and bind the rather pulpy end result to a hook with shirring elastic. What you then have bears no resemblance to a crab whatsoever. It dangles at the end of the line like Houdini, in one of those stunts where he was straitjacketed, tied up with rope, and suspended by his feet from a crane. But to the bass of the Sussex coast, the scent of the crab parcel you have just made is as irresistible as that of a freshly baked loaf to a hungry man.

After half an hour I had lacerated hands, wet feet (the waders I had borrowed from my brother leaked), and one bait. I cast it out very carefully, a gentle lob of about twenty yards into the gully which separated me from the three sharp jags of rock known as the Dragon's Teeth. I was astonished to get a bite more or less immediately. In my surprise, however, I failed to loosen the clutch on the reel, the rod doubled and the line, quickly stretched taut, snapped as it rubbed against the rocks at the gully's edge. I scrounged some more bait, and fished on. Another bite, and this time, although the rod again bent nearly double when I struck, I failed to hook the fish at all. The morning wore on, the tide came in, we went to the pub. Fishless, we plotted the evening's campaign.

So it was that, a few hours later, we walked down the track to the Mere. A blazing hot afternoon was cooling into a balmy evening. The sea had a bit of movement, and the water was milky with suspended grains of chalk. Ideal conditions for bass, which would be swimming in with the tide, hunting by scent the small creatures that lived in the jumble of boulders which lined the beach. The less visibility there was in the water, the better the chances of the fish being drawn to the crab parcels. This time it was easier to find bait. I was beginning to learn what to look for. I could soon spot crabs buried in sand so that only the small circle of shell was exposed which they needed to breathe through (or whatever it is that they do). I could tell almost at a glance the ones which were about to shed their shells, as they had a paler, more mottled, complexion. Within a short time I had enough bait to last the entire tide.

The fishing at the Mere is rather easier than at the Dragon's Teeth. You stand on a rocky platform on one side of a beach, above the boulders, and cast a short distance onto clean sand. A hooked fish can run a long way from you, without the danger of dragging your line around outcrops of rock. This enables you to fish with more sporting tackle than that necessary for the strong-arm tactics of the reefs. I borrowed a lighter rod, and a small multiplier filled with twelve pound line. I changed baits frequently, to keep the level of scent up.

The sun was setting when I felt the first, tentative double tap on the rod tip which shows that a bass is interested in your bait. I waited. The evening had grown cooler, and although I had been shivering, I stopped. It is curious that the body can tense up completely when it needs to, without any conscious prompting. There was a long pause, when not a muscle moved. Then the rod tip was dragged around, I struck, and the fish was on. It headed away from the rocks, picking up speed, and stripping line from the clutch as in all the best fishing stories. I had only caught small school bass before, and although they had fought gamely, they had not prepared me for the sheer power of one of their elders and betters. I kept my

head, and the fish settled into a pattern of short runs, interspersed with periods of head shaking, rather like a pike. And, like a pike, it eventually came to the surface, some way out to sea, and although I could only just make it out, the sight of its massive tail thrashing the water made me realise that it was worth taking care over. As I began to gain line, I relaxed a little until I remembered that the net was some distance away, with my brother. To beach the fish would have involved a tricky walk backwards over quickly filling gullies and loose rocks. I yelled for assistance. My brother shouted back that there was no need to worry, I should just pull the fish out by sticking my fingers under its gill covers. I said I did not think that would be possible. It was too big.

The fish, docile now, was a few feet away. Only then did I really notice the rock between it and me. I yelled again, rather more frantically, and my brother finally picked up the net and came awards me. But, in shouting, I had let my concentration lapse, and somehow, fate being what it is, the line had become caught on the rock. The fish, beaten, lay on the surface like a Chinese kite, tethered to the rock and streaming out with the movement of the tide.

I gently pulled on the line, hoping to free it, but it would not budge. In desperation, I tugged harder. Then the inevitable happened. The hook hold, already loosened during the fight, gave way under the weight of the fish in the tide. The hook sprang clear, the fish hung in the water, tantalisingly close but just out of reach. Then, realising it was free, it slowly, agonisingly, sank from sight. I stared after it. There was no point in feeling upset, none in feeling angry. I just felt empty. A short, sharp expletive, and I packed up my gear, to face the long trudge back to the car.

A week later, I faced the examiners for my viva. After initial courtesies, they began to question me on my Old English literature paper. 'Tell me, Mr Haywood, what was Beowulf clutching when he emerged from the mere?' The mere? The Mere? My mind tried to focus on the blood-stained, turbid water in a dark, dismal wood which was home for the monster Grendel and his mother. But it was a hot day, and very difficult to concentrate. Mention of the Mere took me back to quite a different monster, in turbid water that was chalk-stained, under a clear, balmy sky. I got a Second.

So, instead of becoming an academic, I joined the army, swapping the claustrophobic libraries for the open training areas of Wales and Norfolk, and exchanged my digs in a shortly-to-be-renovated town house known as The Pit, for rooms in a seventeenth century mansion in Wiltshire which had its own trout lake. In the process, I met and married a young WRAC officer. This more than made up for the other blow that I suffered that summer. The St. Anne's girl, during my trip to Sussex, had left me for a theologian, albeit one who was about to test the theory about camels and the eyes of needles by making his fortune in a merchant bank.

These other events put the loss of the big bass in perspective. The mind can devise ways of coping with disappointments of ambition, or of the heart, and swiftly accepts that these things usually turn out for the best. But it can do nothing about a fish that gets away. You see, it is almost certain that I will never catch a bigger one, for a lost fish has an elasticity which, in the imagination, makes it bigger than anything you can ever catch afterwards. You will never know just how big it was.

Nor does it matter. I have caught many bass since, some large, one or two memorable. But nothing lives in my memory quite like that massive silver fish, sinking slowly out of sight, just beyond my reach.

CHAPTER TWO

LAST CAST ON DAL HARRALD

Max Hastings

To cast a fly all day for salmon without touching a fish can be a frustrating business – a dreary one, if the experience is repeated on the morrow. But, as I become a more experienced fisher, I comfort myself by rationalising the matter. Looking through my gamebook since I caught my first salmon fifteen years ago, I find that ever since (and excluding Alaska), I have averaged just over a fish a day. That is better than many men are fortunate enough to achieve, not because I am a good fisher, but because I am lucky enough to cover some good rivers in good weeks. But then consider three or four autumn days last year, on each of which I caught four, five, six fish. How many blank days now await me, before the relentless averages catch up again!

I thought as much during three happy but empty days on the Spey in the spring, and I am not too confident about the Laxford in August. But all of us who pursue salmon accept the inevitability of some outright failures – when there is no water or too much, and when there are simply no fish running through the beat, or the sun is too bright. How much more painful, though, than failing to glimpse fish, is to see them, to rise them, to hook them – and then to find them gone. The mirror image of that moment of ecstasy when one lifts a fish from the water in the net is that alpine descent into anti-climax and emptiness when the line goes slack, the rod straightens, the fly appears on the surface once more, trailing its slender wake across the current to the bank.

What did I do wrong? Did I exert too much pressure? Should I use less check on the old reel? Should I have moved more readily down the bank with the fish? Almost every fisherman sinks into a protracted agony of self-reproach in those awful minutes after a fish has gone, searching his soul to ask what he could have done differently. To fail to touch a fish can be largely attributed to luck (as long as no one else on the beat is faring any better). But to hook a fish, and then to let it go – that is failure; or so it seems to all of us when it happens.

In reality, of course, chance plays as big a part in whether one lands a hooked fish as in every other aspect of fishing. There are plenty of rivers like the Shin, with its steep, narrow gorges, where if a good fish decides to rush downstream, the bravest and most athletic of rods can be left with no means of pursuing it.

There are the days we all know, when fish are taking short. Again and again, a salmon proves lightly hooked in the lip, and breaks away at the first leap. My heart always sinks when I feel a 'head banger' on the end of the rod, one of those fish that begins

systematically to jerk at the fly beneath the surface. So often, the 'head hangers' never reach the net.

But most of us can also remember plenty of fish which we know we should have landed, if we had not made idiotic mistakes. One afternoon after shooting, I ran across the field down to the Findhorn, to get an hour's casting on the falling river, before I was due to catch the train south. Within five minutes, I was into a good fish. Within two more, I was wretchedly fingering the twist of nylon at the end of the cast, from which fly and fish had parted. I knew that salmon had escaped only because I had tied a hasty, careless knot.

Gillies have often reproached me for playing fish too hard, and especially for being in too much of a hurry to bring them to the net. I am never sure about this argument, because I think plenty of fish are also lost by being too lightly handled, allowed to worry the fly all over the river for fifteen minutes before they break free, when they might have been on the bank in ten. Most of the fishermen I admire handle salmon sensitively, but rigorously.

I don't think I am much different from other rods, when I say that I can remember almost every fish I have ever lost, with much greater clarity than fish I have landed. Those moments of bitter disappointment are photographed and retained in the brain's album, from the Syre pool on the Naver in high summer, to a snowbound November morning on the Tweed.

One afternoon at the end of September, I had been fishing the Naver all day in high water, with a sink-tip line and a three-inch Waddington's. It was windy and intermittently showery, and my casting had not been seen to great advantage by John, the young gillie. At 9am, it looked as if the level was falling, and I fancied we should be in for a good day, on my favourite Beat 1. But we thrashed Dal Mallart and the Stables and Dal Harrald, hour after hour in vain. I had caught my fly as often as usual in the cables of the hanging bridge across Dal Harrald, and collected my customary expansive collection of wind knots. John was surprised that we didn't meet a fish, but maybe rather less so than he would have been, had I been throwing a better line. My hands were wet and aching on the rod butt. I love all those Sutherland rivers, but the Naver perhaps best of any.

Yet, by late afternoon, I was growing tired and cross and frustrated. Why could I never winkle a fish out of Dal Mallart, which always looks the finest pool on the river, and where more fish show than in any other? A couple of years back, I got as far as hooking one, and hearing my son say, 'Well done, Daddy', before it was off and gone. Today, I had flogged it twice, maybe even three times, to no purpose. Why, in all that great expanse of heavy water in the pools below, was there not one fish which would take me? John announced that it was time for him to go home, and we fixed the rendezvous for next morning.

I sat on the bank for a few minutes, resting over a cigar. Much as I value the indispensable advice of gillies about the lie of the pools, I usually fish better alone. I become less self-conscious about my tangles. I concentrate more.

Ten minutes later, I landed an eight-pounder in the Lower Stables, hooked just where I would expect to find him, where a swollen burn runs down from the hill into the river.

It was only five o'clock. The only constraints on the fishing now were my wet clothes and my tiredness. I drove back up to Dal Harrald, and crossed the river by the bridge. We had not yet fished the pool from the far side. In the gusting wind, conditions were less than ideal, with the trees and steep bank and deep heather to create all the circumstances for me to make a fool of myself. But, when better places have failed, try the less obvious ones. Pace by pace, I began to work wearily down the pool.

By six, I was exhausted. The rain and wind had come on again. Only ten yards of fishable water to go. Pack it in? Oh, what the hell. I felt doggedly determined to finish what I had started. Ten minutes later, I made a last cast into the streamy water at the tail of the pool. The line straightened, and began to swim away from me. In an instant, tiredness evaporated. All my senses were electrified, as I tensed to respond. I lifted the rod point, wound line fast onto the reel, and tightened on the fish, revelling in the reward for persistence.

The salmon tore away across the river, taking line. I stood my ground on the bank, the 15-foot Bruce and Walker well bent in my hands. On the far side, perhaps thirty yards out, it checked and began to swim towards me. I reeled in steadily, confident that we were well connected. Then, under my own bank in the blustery drizzle, the fish turned once more, and sprang away downstream, the reel screaming in that irresistible fashion. I let it run, and run. It had gone perhaps thirty yards back across the stream, and as many below me, when as I watched the backing slipping out through the rod rings, I had a sudden flash of knowledge that this was an uncommonly strong, uncommonly big fish for the Naver.

I knew pretty well what a 10-pounder felt like, or a 12-pounder. This must be bigger than that. Fifteen? Sixteen? The Tay or Tweed would laugh at me for growing excited about a fish of this size. But up here, in the remote fastness of Sutherland, you judge by what you expect. Six or eight pounds is average or above, on this stretch of water. Belatedly, I grasped that more responsive tactics were needed, and began to stumble as rapidly as I could down the rocky bankside, reeling hard as I went. The salmon was far out in heavily broken water now, moving powerfully. I splashed across the mouth of a peaty little burn, spewing foamy water into the main stream.

The fish paused in the current, and I seized the moment to throw away the strap of my wading staff, get my net off my shoulder and extend it. Any fish landed alone seems worth two in which a gillie has a hand, not because I do not value and admire gillies, but because lone achievement in any sport gives a special pleasure. The fish eased towards me, five yards, ten, fifteen. Then it was tearing away once more, down and across the stream. Five yards short of the far bank it stopped. The waves seemed to batter my taut line. My heart sank.

With relentless jerks, the fish began to tug at me once, twice, three times. I glanced at my watch. Almost 15 minutes gone since I hooked it. There was one more sharp wrench. Then the line came free, and the fly bounced back across the water towards me.

I sank back onto the bank, utterly disconsolate. After hours of effort and patience, a quarter of an hour of intense excitement, I was staring at failure. All my tiredness came back. I became once more conscious of my sopping Barbour jacket and Husky, the water trickling down my neck. I wound in the line, and trudged slowly back up the pool to the bridge, the car, and the lodge.

All the way, of course, I turned over in my mind not my success at the Lower Stables, but my failure at Dal Harrald. The gripping mystery, the enigma of that occasion, as of so much salmon fishing, was that never once in my fight had I glimpsed that salmon. I had felt his power, seen the line tearing out and the rod arched towards the river to meet him. But I did not know, could never know, what manner and size of fish I had met, struggled with, and lost. Could he have been as much as twenty pounds? I doubt it, on the Naver. Could he have been one of those small fish which sometimes fight so formidably, often harder than their big brethren? I think not – there was real weight behind that pull from the depths of the current. Was there anything I should have done differently? Yes – I should have handled him more gently, followed him down the bank as soon as he began to run, rather than idly attempting to handle him where I had hooked him.

I had made the fatal mistake of being blasé with him, of regarding him as just another fish, rather than as I should, with the care and commitment and passionate concentration one bestows upon the first fish of the week, of the year, of one's life. All salmon are special. Each one deserves the utmost attention and respect. If the respect is lacking, so also will be the fish. I caught a dozen salmon in the next two days. But the one I remember now, which nags at my memory and my conscience and my pride, is the fish I lost that first day in Dal Harrald. What was it, how was it hooked? Part of the perverse magic and beauty of fishing is that I shall be forever ignorant.

CHAPTER THREE

TOO SOON AN AGE

Brian Clarke

There is a critical point in the life of an angler which comes, if it is to come at all, at the moment he first translates his mind beneath the water's surface.

After that moment, which can come at any time and which came relatively late to me, the rational takes over. He begins to think clinically. Because of the acidity of that lake, fish are unlikely to grow larger than so. Fish of a particular species will certainly not exceed the other. This water will contain whoppers. They will be in the deeps, in the shallow, on the top, near the bottom because, because.

This kind of knowledge makes for absorbing angling. It leads to intellectual and tactical challenges of a thousand kinds and to much thought and experimentation even away from the bankside. But it is a different kind of fishing to that practised before the moment of revelation.

In those earlier, more innocent days, the line does not link the hand and the brain behind it with known possibilities and likelihoods.

In the age of innocence, the line is a fine-drawn nerve. Out there it disappears into a restless deep; here it roots into the imagination behind the bright-wide eyes. It transmits images and excitements and awe, perhaps even a little dread. And so a fish lost in that age when anything might live has no form and no size because clinical thoughts and reason have not yet intervened.

The loss – the effects of loss, the scars the loss creates – go so much deeper in the young. The loss at the age of twelve of a fish of awful proportions is a damaging thing. The more so, I think, when the fish is a pike. A pike! Clouds gather. Lightning strikes. Rocks split open!

My own leviathan lost was a pike. It is a loss that has marked me for an angling lifetime even though, years later, in a faded cutting about its eventual captor, I was to learn its weight to the ounce.

It was a midsummer's afternoon. The sun burned like a brazier overhead. Bees drowsed. Flowers drooped. Cattle acquiesced beneath shading oaks.

Dace dimpled.

I had made my way upstream from the old stone bridge at Croft, on the Tees near Darlington, spinning for trout and chub with a small quill minnow. My rod was cheap split cane. My reel was an inexpensive fixed-spool. I was in short trousers. Black wellingtons flapped at my knees.

I was prospecting; dropping the quill minnow into every likely place in the weak-tea, North-country water. The bottom was mostly flat ledges of rock and it was to the clefts and steps of the rock that instinct, rather than knowledge, had me aim.

The rod end was flicked, the quill minnow described shallow arc though the air, there was a muted plop and the bale-arm clicked over. Wind.

And so it went, searching, trying, checking, double-checking. Flick, arch, plop, click, wind. Flick, arch, plop, click, wind.

When I was just opposite the mouth of the River Skerne, where it entered the Tees alongside tables of rock we all knew as 'the ledges', I saw another ridge on the river bed.

Flick, arch, plop, click, wind. The minnow had landed a little too far downstream. Flick again, arch, plop. Perfect. The minnow went in just above the ridge on the rock and a little to the far side of it. I allowed it to settle for a moment, clicked over the bale-arm, and began to wind again.

But nothing. For the second or third time that afternoon, I had snagged heavily. I lifted the little rod to my right shoulder and pumped carefully. I put the rod to my left shoulder and pumped again. No movement. I moved upstream a few paces and downstream a few paces, trying again. No movement.

I pulled a little harder. The water toyed with the light, reflecting it here, slipping it there. The line played a highly-strung, oriental tune. But still nothing.

Eventually – and it was a serious decision in those far-off days, when everything was funded by an early-morning paper round, when hooks were counted, short lengths of line were knotted and a quill minnow took two days up garden paths to buy – eventually, I pointed the rod down the line and began to pull to break.

Something shifted.

I tightened the nut that tightened the clutch slightly, and pulled as hard as I dared. And then I saw whatever it was I was snagged into, begin to lift. It was like a drowned log. But no angular arm broke the surface, no cloud of silt drifted downstream.

It is the breaking of the surface that has haunted me. It took long seconds, like some slow, mental dawning. There was a gathering of shades, a convergence of colours, a suggestion of distinctions.

And then the pike's skull was there like an electric shock, paralysing the bright afternoon.

There were the marble eyes, the sprung-trap jaws, the lean, mottled flanks and the far-away, orange, great oars of the tail. I saw all of it, every bit of it, little by little as the fish came up and the water peeled away like ancient time. I was raising the unspoken from my own imagination.

The pike lay on the surface for several moments, as though to convince me it was real. And then it shrugged, turned its head down and swam to the far side of the river. I cannot put it more dramatically than that. There was no effort involved. There was no thrashing of the water. It did not run or dash. It simply swam heavily, irresistibly, to the opposite bank.

Then it swam back. Then it swam to the other side of the river again. Then it returned.

On the seventh crossing of the river, with the fish headed dead away from me, the clutch on the tiny reel jammed, my arm and rod were educated to the horizontal, and the line broke.

Again, there were no dramatics. It did not part with a sound like a pistol shot, it simply broke with a disappointing, low-key switch, as though an elastic band, lightly stretched, had been released. The last visible suggestion of the fish sank away.

I could not believe what had happened. For perhaps a minute or more I stood there, sightlessly staring, held in a kind of emotional death. Then I reeled slowly in and made leadenly to the bank. My companions on 'the ledges' had seen all of it, could scarcely believe they had seen any of it.

The line was 3 lbs breaking strain. The pike weighed 21¼ lbs.

Twelve is too soon an age for such a thing to happen.

CHAPTER FOUR

THE FISH BY THE THISTLE

Sidney Vines

loyd Vient was about sixty years old and made of whipcord. He was my fishing guide when I fished Lake Diamond and Diamond Creek in the South Island of New Zealand.

'If you want some good fishing, away from the crowds,' said the owner of the motel in Queenstown where my wife and I were staying, 'go to Paradise, at the far end of Lake Wakatipu and stay with the Millers. I'll phone them and they'll put you up. Duggie Campbell has a car and he'll drive you down. OK? Good as gold.'

So easily are things arranged in New Zealand. Duggie Campbell came the next day and we hired him for the drive of about thirty miles. Queenstown is at the west end of Lake Wakatipu and Paradise is at the east end. Like every New Zealand taxi driver I met, he had a rod in his boot and showed signs of wanting to stop off along the way and fish the lake. We wanted to get to Paradise and settle in, so I dissuaded him.

The scenery in this part of New Zealand bears an uncanny resemblance to the Scottish Highlands, but on a grander scale. The mountains rise to 10,000 feet, the rivers and lakes are bigger, but it has the same feel of clean cold, beauty as, say, Wester Ross. Near the east end of Wakatipu we passed the village of Glenorchy, with a shop, a church, a school, a cluster of nondescript wooden bungalows, and a landing strip for light aircraft. 'Glenorchy International Airport,' said Duggie as we passed.

Paradise, about three miles further, was a hamlet of only three houses. It lay in a green and fertile valley about a mile wide, with the mountains towering up on either side. This is sheep country, and they grazed in their thousands along the valley and on the lower slopes. The Millers were a charming couple with two children aged eight and ten. They installed us in a guest bungalow and cooked us supper al fresco under the eucalyptus trees.

They made a wood fire, wrapped some lamb chops in foil, and cooked them in the embers. We sat at a rough table under the trees and ate them, while a large silver-breasted New Zealand robin looked on. They must have liked us, for they asked if we would keep an eye on their children for the next couple of days, while they went on a visit to Dunedin. Imagine an English couple leaving their children for two days to the care of complete strangers!

After supper, David Miller told me that my guide the next day would be Lloyd Vient, a retired farmer, who lived close by. He would come at 9am with his Land Rover and sandwiches and

30

beer: all I had to do was be ready. When we arrived at Paradise, in the early afternoon, I had taken a walk with my wife through the eucalyptus trees to Diamond Lake. We stood in the heat of the sun (it was February, equivalent to August in the northern hemisphere) admiring five square miles of crystal clear water. The sun burnt down. In England the trout would have been lying on the bottom, but here, to my surprise, the fish were moving. I would return after supper, I thought, for the evening rise. But when, in the cool of the evening, I did return, rod in hand, the rise had stopped. Lloyd Vient later explained that in New Zealand there was no evening rise. Fish rose all day, even in days of heat.

Next day, Lloyd arrived and said that we were going to fish the lake first, and then the creek. We drove a mile or so, to the lake shore, and I tackled up and put on chest waders. 'We're going to wade across the lake,' said Lloyd, 'for about half a mile – it's only about three feet deep – to where you see that large log. Beyond it is the stream running into Diamond Creek, and that is where the fish are.' I knew they would be browns, for there are hardly any rainbows in the South Island.

'How big?'

'About four pounds, eating beetles and grasshoppers off the surface. Put on a Coch y Bondhu. And don't get too near.'

I digested this information while I put on the fly, thinking how odd it was that a traditional Welsh fly should be the choice, here on the other side of the world. Also, looking at the perfect clarity of the water, it was obvious that fine and far off was the message – but not too fine, for wild four pounders!

31

We set off together, wading across the lake. It was hard work, for the bottom was soft mud, and at each step I sank up to my knees. However, I made progress. Lloyd, his own rod up, was about fifty yards away. When I was short of the log, I over-balanced backwards. It was tiredness, I suppose, after half an hour's steady wading though that gooey mud. At any rate, down I went, and found myself sitting in the water up to my chest with both legs firmly embedded in the mud, quite unable to move. I felt like Carver Doone on Exmoor, slowly sinking into the quicksand. My past transgressions flashed before me, and I regretted there had not been a few more of them.

But Lloyd, slimmer and fitter than me, was over in a moment to give a helping hand and put me back on my feet. Of course, a wading stick would have been the answer. Three legs are better than two, and I have never since gone wading where conditions are difficult without one. The mishap over, we arrived at the log, and I saw the fish. There were several of them – magnificent silvery fellows, like small salmon. I stayed well away, behind the log, and the cast was about twenty yards. I took two, both on Coch y Bondhus, and finer dry fly fishing you could not want.

We returned to the Land Rover without further incident and had our lunch. Lloyd said a wise thing: 'If one day in four is a fly fishing day, you are doing well.' 'You are right, Lloyd,' I replied, 'and this is a fly fishing day.' He grinned. 'And it isn't over yet.' My spirits rose at the thought of the triumphs that lay ahead. The possibility of disaster never entered my head.

After lunch, at peace with the world, I asked Lloyd how

it came about that the settlement was called Paradise, and he told the story, which went as follows. When Queenstown was first established, in the 1860s, a young Scot called Andrew Duncan – a romantic youth, like Bonnie Prince Charlie – was sent out with a mob of sheep (in New Zealand they always talk of a 'mob' of sheep) to found a settlement at the far end of Lake Wakatipu. This he did, and there he met a Maori wahine, or maiden. 'What are you going to call this place?' she asked. 'As long as I am with you, it is Paradise,' he replied. So it became, and so it has remained.

Lloyd said we would now fish Diamond Creek, the stream that took the waters of Diamond Lake into Wakatipu. We drove around to the mouth and began to walk carefully upstream. The banks were steep, of hard sand, four feet above the water which flowed strong and clear. After about twenty minutes, Lloyd stopped and pointed. There the trout lay, on our side of the river, about thirty yards above us, under a thistle – not an anaemic English thistle, but a bristling Scottish thistle in full purple flower. I gazed at him, and held my breath in awe, at his grace, power, and beauty. He must have been at least six pounds.

In whispers, we discussed tactics. The only feasible way to tackle that fish was to go back down to the bottom, where there was a footbridge, cross, come up the other bank, and slide down to a sandy patch about twenty yards below the fish, from where a good cast would put the fly in front of him.

So while Lloyd stayed to observe, I carried out the plan until I was standing on the sandy patch ready to cast. It had taken about half an hour. My heart was in my mouth, for I reckoned I had only one chance. It was a long throw. It had to be accurate, and it had to be delicate for in that clear water he could see everything, as I could see his gills opening and closing. Concentrating all my mind, I cast, and wonder of wonders, it landed perfectly, three feet above his nose. He saw it, and his whole massive body tilted upwards, his jaws opened – and I struck, pulling the fly straight out of his mouth.

The fish turned and saw me. He looked full at me with an expression of fury and disdain, as if to say: 'How dare you! What have I done to you?' Then, in full dignity, he departed upsteam, and I, like the Psalmist, 'by the waters of Diamond Creek, lay down and wept.'

From my records, I see that later that day I caught two more large fish but I can remember nothing of them. It is the fish by the thistle that remains in my memory, and will do so to the end of my days.

CHAPTER FIVE

WHEN ALL THE WORLD WAS YOUNG

David Street

I am sometimes asked what strange alchemy it was that turned me – an apparently rational fellow – into a lifelong fisherman. One might imagine that, by now, I would have my answer off pat, but that is not the way it is. My reply can never be immediate, for the very question seems to pre-empt all normal, logical thought. For a time, I lapse into reverie, while an inner ear listens in again to a music I first heard, as a young boy, beside a mountain stream and, ever since, have carried with me all my life. When, at last, I do attempt an answer, I am greeted by blank stares or smiles of pity – esotericism is scarcely the rage – and there are some who even surmise that I must be touched. They, perhaps, are right.

This beguiling river of my first delight was spawned in the dark bosom of the Mynydd Dolgoed, high on a desolate wetland, where the lilt of curlew and the drumming of snipe alone hailed her birth. A chuckle of unseen waters, tinkling in deep runnels, betrays the mighty torrent that is yet to be. New-sprung, the stream breaks from her highland cradle and, greeting the sun with a skip and a frolic, shows herself in peacock tails of amber, clear as ale.

She follows now an ancient course, one quarried out for her by trolls in a primeval morning of the world. Here, on myriad looms of rock, she starts to weave her infinite patterns of enchantment. Rippling shallows, racing, white-tipped, lead on to a gentler glide, where waters, thrusting hard at haphazard boulders, divide and, swirling to either side, form quiet, enticing eddies, mosaic-pebbled on floors of sand; sinuous, her fingers search each secret recess, now curling in and out of moss-grown banks, undercut, yet bound by root of alder which, here, over-arch the stream to form a cathedral-cloistered pool in dappled shade; closing, at last, towards her consummation, she quickens pace and, with a splendour of abandon, plunges, in spray of rainbows, to the seething cauldron of a deep-chiselled pool, twenty feet below. My river's course is all but run – a few hundred yards and her genius is finally and trustingly surrendered to the broader sweeps of the river Dovey.

Such then, in cameo, was the blithe stream, some five miles in length, which, in holidays from boarding school before the war, first cast the spell upon me and planted, within, that particular vein of poetry that sealed me for a fisherman.

Our house stood on the side of a hill, two hundred yards above the little river and over halfway down her course. As I lay awake there in my bed, revelling in that delectable no-man's land that lies between tiredness and sleep, and already planning tomorrow's exploits, I would listen in to the voices of the night, beyond my window. The tawny owl would call; a dog fox bark; lambs, astray, bleating for their dams; the soft sighing of breezes, at play in the tops of the tall cypress that fanned the moon; all evocative sounds, superimposing themselves upon the one, constant tintinnabulation of dancing waters, which, in times of spate, became a roar that filled the valley, rising to the rim of the hills.

It was a time for me to dream my dreams, often nourished by the wild voices; a time to build my castles in the air. At thirteen, my imagination owned few bounds, delighting in whimsy and hatching her own chimeras; it was an age when reality and myth were intertwined; an age to be in love with life, when fantasies could turn to fact, and even the wildest dreams might see the light of day.

Throughout the years of adolescence, I spent many days wandering the banks of my river, alone with my thoughts, and carrying my seven-foot, spit-cane, Farlow's rod and wicker creel. These were, indeed, the halcyon days, for the genial river beckoned and I had all the world to learn. We had much in common and, between us, there built a powerful empathy. Together we shared our youth, revealed our secrets; her energies were mine; our destinies all unknown, we yet were happy in the day itself.

I loved her then for what she was and, in return, she taught me all the ways of trout, how to stalk them and observe them; how to make use of sun and cloud, the wind and trees and, above all, the play of water upon rock and bank. I came to know those places where the fish would lie and, especially those spots where the best of them would be found. Then, it was a matter of landing a fly, or dropping a worm, with the accuracy of a marksman and the delicacy of a ballerina. Few, if any, second chances were afforded and mistakes went unrewarded. With every twist and turn she took, the river showed fresh patterns, repositioning the pieces on the chessboard and opening up a whole new set of challenges. As I worked my way upstream, I learnt to adapt my skill to the requirements of each and every pool. Did ever a boy have a finer teacher, or the burn a more devoted pupil?

By the age of twelve, I could come home in the evening with a bag of trout, and all of them keepers. What treasure these game little fish were, with their dark backs and bright, jewelled flanks, that reflected the gold of the sunlight. Fried in butter, with a rasher of home-cured bacon from the farm and fresh-picked mushrooms from the meadow, here was a breakfast fit for all angling neophytes and other winsome lads. Just occasionally, I might catch one that was two inches longer and weighed a full quarter of a pound, and he would be about as big as the little burn afforded.

Fishermen tend to make a fetish out of size, as though the quality of a trout resides in his inches or in his ounces, whereas we should look to find it in his own innate beauty, the splendour of his rising and the spirited sport that he provides.

These little burn trout were destined to remain small and stunted, because their food supply was always scant and their home frequently scoured by floods. If they were the humble yeomen of the trout world, content to live their lives within the jejune pastures of their inheritance, then their brother trout – the sewin – answered to a different spirit. They were the buccaneers, ready to quit the familiar horizons of their homesteads to seek their fortunes on the broad expanses of the ocean, where many perils and unimaginable riches lay before them.

Then, at length, summoned by the stimulus to spawn, they return on a summer's tide to the very estuary by which they left, and so up the main river to the junction pool. There, they rest awhile, until freshening pulses in the water's flow disturb their lethargy, and send their bodies quivering in thrills of new excitement. Now, endowed with the leaper's prowess and flexing those muscles with which the sea has furnished them, they turn aside and nose their way into the expanding torrent of the burn, to begin the ascent to their ancestral nurseries in the hills.

In my river, those marvellous fish were the nonpareil, without peer, the very stuff of dreams. They were, however, seldom glimpsed except in times of spate, when they would hurl themselves heavenwards against the full fury of the falls. Yet, they still seemed to belong more to sportive fancy than to actuality, to inhabit not so much the river as the mind, which they haunted with a wistful longing.

When I fished for brownies, I would set out in the delightful assurance of sport, conscious only that I was an initiate, a growing master, not merely of the art but also the science of my craft. With the sewin, however, that was not so, for I was not yet in their league. It seemed to me, then, that they belonged almost entirely to the world of adults and to the realms of darkness; to men who wielded long rods, wading the wide waters of the Dovey on nights when the moon was hid; or to those bolder, and more rascally, lads than I, who, in the witching hour, prowled the banks of the burn with their lamps and spears; all times, when young boys were abed and dreaming.

On the fateful day, I was making my way home after fishing the lower reaches, and had paused beside the main waterfall pool. It lay just off the long drive to the one big house in the valley and, in earlier years, the owners had built a gazebo and viewing platform here, together with railings to prevent children falling some twenty feet onto the rocks below. It was a favourite haunt of mine, not just for the grandstand view it gave of mighty fish leaping, when the spate ran high, but because there was always much to see. Sprightly dippers, those guardian spirits of the rollicking waters, nested here beneath the falls, and the burn trout were always entertaining, in constant motion to inspect for food. It was as I was watching them that I caught sight of a pair of sewin, in full livery of sea-silver, swimming, with measured fin, around the perimeters of the pool, in deep water well below the trout.

Suddenly, the old familiar place shone with the brightness of a glory I had not seen before. A great excitement and delight now flooded through me, as I wondered at the grace and power with which they swam all through the pool, dwarfing the trout that once had been their peers. I gazed at them for a full ten minutes, until they disappeared from sight somewhere in the wild turbulence at the pool's head. I would have been happy just to go on gazing and marvelling but, as the vision faded, so atavistic memories stirred within, and I knew the river was summoning to her greatest adventure yet.

I had in my pocket a tin of brandling worms, but I needed something bigger now. I knew that Price the Paper's son was fishing eels from the bridge downstream, and I decided to see if I could cadge a couple of blackheads from him, without letting on that I was after sewin. This achieved, I returned to the platform, mounted the worm on my Pennell tackle and lobbed it into the white waters. I then stood the rod against the railings, pausing to invoke the immortals to smile upon my thirteen years.

Apprehension, terrible both in its longing and its trepidation, seized me now; how could I land a sewin from this pinnacle of rock beyond the railings, and without a net, for tyros did not carry nets? Were I to hook him, play and lose him, who would believe my story? Such were my forebodings as I waited. The pounding of the falls filled my ears, locking me irrevocably into this cauldron of decision. It was now or never. Reaching down for the rod, I began to raise it very slowly, sensing for the worm on the bed of the stream. Then, with a crash bang wallop, my rod became a living entity in my hands, thrilling to a new and urgent energy.

To this day, I do not know how I managed to get myself and my rod, with its plunging appendage, down to the river's bank where, at least, we could fight on some kind of terms. In the pool, the sewin played hard and long, his head down and boring deep into every corner and recess. Then, in a sudden change of tactics, he surfaced and, using the race in the outflow, he slipped the pool and made off downstream in a spirited run, stripping line for all his worth. To follow him now, I had no real option but to join him in the river, where I measured my length several times, stumbling on rocks, slippery as eels. We were well below the falls by the time he showed signs of tiring – or so I thought – now rolling and showing the white flash of his underbelly. I started to increase the pressure, to ease him out of the current and towards a shelving bank of gravelly shingle, but he had another run in mind which he accomplished and then crowned with a triumphant leap of glory – to freedom.

At that age, I was obviously very disappointed, but why – only because I had no corpse to display at home, no visible proof except my mien and my scars? In truth, I had lost nothing but gained much, an experience enriching me well beyond my years. Does not Father Izaak tell us that no man can lose that which he never had; and from the bard himself: 'Let us not burden our remembrances with a heaviness that is gone'? Already the river was extending my discipleship into further fields of wisdom, for angling by its very nature tends towards philosophy.

There will, I fear, be some readers who want to know how heavy my fish was, while I, for my part, want to know by what canons a boy's first fish is to be judged. I suppose, looking back over more than half a century, he weighed a pound, or perhaps half as much again, but that is not his measure. As a statement, it tells nothing of my sewin, but merely reduces him to a parity with a million others, destroying the uniqueness that is his. I, alone, know his measure and that is the reason I am fishing for his progeny still.

CHAPTER SIX

MISADVENTURE AT MALINDI

Julian Paget

t was 1960 and I was stationed in Kenya with the Army. The Mau Mau troubles were over, and my wife and I had time and a unique opportunity to enjoy some of the magnificent sport that the country had to offer.

This included big game fishing off Malindi, and we were extremely lucky to be taken out on several occasions by that famous angler, H. B. Swan, who was one of the greatest experts in East Africa. As a result we nearly always caught something, usually barracuda or tunny, and if we were fortunate a sailfish of around 100 lbs. It was tremendous fun, particularly as there were few other fishermen about then, and happily no Japanese with their lethal long lines.

On the momentous day we went out at dawn, and Diana and I were both trailing our baits in a calm sea. Diana had the first strike and it was clear that it was something big. It did not jump as a sailfish would but surged away in a powerful, irresistible run of well over a hundred yards.

'It must be a marlin,' said H.B. 'And a big one too.'

I reeled in and we all concentrated on Diana. It was now about 7am, and for a full hour we did not even see the fish. Then it jumped – an awe-inspiring sight. It was a marlin, and a huge one.

For two hours the battle continued, and we were nowhere near getting it alongside. The African boatman, Abdul, manoeuvred the boat skilfully, but the fish simply did not seem to tire.

Then the swivel chair seized up, and Diana could no longer swing round so as to face the fish. There was only one answer, and that was for H.B. and myself to lift the whole chair, including Diana, and move it round whenever she had to change direction. It was extremely hard work, and made it that much harder for Diana to play the fish properly, but she hung on grimly.

It was now eleven o'clock, and we had been at it for four hours. The sun was almost overhead, and the heat was intense. There was no cooling breeze and the glare off the water was inescapable. Diana was, not surprisingly, becoming exhausted, but we poured water over her, and kept her supplied with cool drinks; and at least the fish was tiring too.

At long last the monster was actually brought to the surface, and we could see it, a mere ten yards from the boat. It was a magnificent blue marlin, well hooked, but very far from defeated.

'That must be all of 600 pounds,' said H.B, and he knew. 'That would be a woman's world record, I think – if we can land it.'

But how? It was now almost alongside, and it was nearly as

long as the boat. Every time it pulled away, we had to let it run, such was the weight and power of the creature. Then Diana would slowly heave it back again, yard by yard. We wanted to take over and give Diana a break, but H.B. said that if we so much as touched the rod or reel, it would not then count as a record because we would have 'assisted' the angler. Quite apart from that, Diana was determined to land the fish by herself.

There was no hope of gaffing it, and in any case we could never have pulled it aboard. H.B. decided that the only hope was to tail it, as one might a salmon. Then, perhaps, we could tow it backwards, which would drown it.

But it would be tricky and any error could snap the line. For at least another hour we heaved on that damned chair, while Diana pumped line, and Abdul manoeuvred the boat. By now half a dozen other boats had converged, having heard word of the battle over their radios, and they sat in a circle, watching, but keeping well clear.

Now the fish was alongside. I manned the chair, while H.B. prepared a rope noose at the end of a boathook for slipping over the great tail from behind. Holding our breath, we all watched.

'If he rushes off, for goodness sake, don't try to stop him,' instructed H.B. 'Let him go.'

He edged the noose into the water, but it just would not go where he wanted. Time and again it was almost there, but the marlin edged away. Then the noose touched the fish. There was an explosion of spray, it lunged away and plunged downwards. The rod was almost pulled out of Diana's hands, and she all but went overboard. As she lost her balance momentarily, the line looped just once round the top ring. No one could reach to free it. After five hours, disaster was just a second away.

The rod bent till it was touching the water. There was a sickening twang, and the line snapped. The huge fish sank very slowly, agonisingly slowly, down into the depths.

H.B. and I were speechless. Diana swore a most unladylike oath, and Abdul burst into tears.

CHAPTER SEVEN

JILTED BY THE QUEEN

Chris Yates

The wonderful emotional storms that an angler experiences when he hooks, plays and then loses an extra-large fish would make an interesting study for a psychologist. First, the tranquillity of the fishing and the passive expectancy as you make your umpteenth cast, then the galvanising shock of contact and the joyous realisation that this is something out of the ordinary. You become light as paper, yet solid as wood. Your heartbeat rises, your vision blurs; there is a steady piling up of hope, yet a constant anxiety; a growing love for whatever creature it is down there, yet a vague terror, like a fear of flying. The longer you have waited the more intense are the emotions; the stronger the fish tussles the more severe your vertigo. And then, at the topmost peak of the world, something terrible happens: the line falls slack

53

and your world splits in two, the disengaged monster diving to the bottom of his pool while you are pitched backwards into an abyss.

It is so outrageous, so unjust, so pathetic. You send up an anguished prayer of complaint to Izaak, but he just wags a disapproving finger as he sits on his celestial creel.

'You cannot lose what you never had!', he says again, just as he argued when the bungling Venator bewailed the loss of a hefty trout. But he is being pedantic. If you have just lost the fish of your dreams you have every right to feel dispossessed. And because you never experienced that final touch that would have made the dream come true, the dream inevitably remains to haunt you.

My own 'List of the Lost' is a long one, beginning when a magnificent carp took unfair advantage of me at a village pond thirty years ago. Moreover, though I have always kept a fishing diary, there was never any need to record all the losses; each moment of separation will always remain etched on my mind. There was a massive, brassy-scaled chub that broke me in the River Mole in 1964 (that still pains me a little for it could have been the biggest chub in the river if not the country, and nowadays there is no possibility of the Mole ever producing such a monster again, so sick has it become with pollution). There was a giant sea-trout that ran me round a rock on a Cumberland river and a fantastic ballan wrasse that showed its glorious coloured flank just once before shimmering down into unyielding kelp and anchoring me immovably. I remember the glimpse I had of a beautiful tench – not a particularly large one – but a fish that would have made an already lovely summer day perfect had it not come suddenly adrift. There

was a colossal barbel, near-record proportions, that ploughed up, across and then down the river, going beyond a great bed of water buttercup and floundering hugely near the surface before slipping the hook. But the biggest and possibly the worst vortex of them all happened when I was jilted by one of Redmire's aristocrats.

Redmire in Herefordshire is (or was, for it is ten years since I fished it regularly) the domain of the largest freshwater fish in Britain. They are all carp.

Though several forty-pounders have been taken there, I have seen fish that were undoubtedly bigger, the largest being so preposterously huge as to seem unbelievable. I saw this giant only once and if it had weighed eighty pounds I wouldn't have been surprised.

I named these aristocrats after chess pieces: there was the King, a fully-scaled fish; the Black Queen, a very dark leather carp of around sixty pounds; the Bishop, a mirror carp of over fifty pounds; two Knights, fully-scaled commons probably in the high forties; the Castle, an ancient-looking mirror carp of between fifty and sixty pounds. Of these six I landed one – the Bishop – in June 1980 and lost another, the Black Queen, in October 1977. This is how it happened.

It was the end of a cool but golden autumn and for the final week of October I had Redmire all to myself. Fishing three days and two nights, though, I caught nothing, not even a small fish and there were no signs of carp feeding. The pool appeared devoid of life and, as the week progressed, the water, normally crystal-clear, seemed to grow darker and more wintery-looking. The willows and poplars shed most of their leaves during a single windy night and only the yellow foliage of the oak remained to give colour to the landscape. At first I fished a pitch on the east bank, but then one grey, calm dawn I saw a brilliant gold flank turn silently on the surface, close to the west bank. It was the sign I was looking for and I moved all my gear round the pool and began fishing a place called Ingham's Pitch. From sunrise to noon, however, nothing came to my baits. Perhaps it was the bait itself that was the problem. I was using prawns, which the carp had enjoyed on my previous visit. But carp are quick to learn and Redmire carp in particular only need one or two of their number to fall for a given bait before they all regard that bait with intense suspicion. It was a good idea to blame the bait. It meant I could do something positive and change it.

I left the pool and drove to Ross where I bought a box of frozen cockles. I had not used cockles before, but I felt the carp might appreciate them as they were, after all, just another form of watersnail, and probably more succulent than the familiar pondsnail. As I drove back to Redmire the clouds lifted and the sun shone for the first time in eight days. Walking round the pond I noticed how much softer and more fragrant the air had become. The water still looked dark, but I felt sure the kinder weather would rouse the sullen fish.

Back at Ingham's I hurled out a few free offerings, cast a bait amongst them, then climbed a tall bankside alder to watch for results. For a while there was nothing but the pale amber plain of the lake bed, flecked by shadows of floating leaves, but then two large grey shapes cruised into view from the deeper water to my right. On they came until they were level with and almost directly below me, but then turned without nosing down for the cockles and dematerialised into the depths again.

After a time, I became aware of a vague cloud of disturbed mud, perhaps four feet across, similar to the cumulus-like boilings thrown up by a carp burrowing for larvae, except that this was less turbid. Almost obscured within it was a dim shape that I presumed was the remains of a dying weed bed. It couldn't possibly have been a fish, as it was simply too big. Gradually, however, the dark form loomed higher in the water, revealing itself as a stupendous blue-black leather carp. At the time it was easily the largest freshwater fish I had ever seen and the clear sight of it made me almost fall out of the tree. I could see the huge pectorals rapidly fanning, unfurling the mud cloud still wider. Then zeppelin-like, it floated forward into clear water, drifting perhaps twenty feet before sinking to the bottom again. With its pectorals it wafted up another thin cloud until it was once more almost wholly obscured.

But I could tell it wasn't bottom-feeding in the normal carp fashion. It seemed to be feeding on whatever it was filtering from the cloud, just as a whale feeds on plankton. In all my years of carp angling I had never seen such behaviour before. For the half hour or so that I watched, the monster rose up, heaved forward and descended again several times, leaving a trail of slowly dissolving clouds in its wake. I was so intrigued that I almost overlooked the fact that the fish had sunk down directly over my bait. Once again, I almost fell out of the tree. Like a dying monkey I slithered and scrambled down the trunk, then crept back to my rod. There was a fold of silver foil over the line and within a few minutes it rustled up to the butt-ring and the loose line began to hiss through it. I struck with reasonable self-control and the reel began to slowly tick off the yards. I knew instantly that it was the monster.

Before that day, I had landed several huge carp including one of forty-three pounds, but none of them felt remotely like the Black Queen. The sensation it gave was of inexhaustible, uncontrollable power, as if I had just hooked a tractor. But Redmire is not a big water, only three acres, and the carp was heading not down its long length but across its width, never more than a hundred yards. Therefore, I told myself to do nothing more than keep in touch, for the monster would soon reach the far bank and I guessed it would then move right, remaining in deep water within my range. Only if it headed left, up towards the distant shallows, would I be in danger of a nervous breakdown. The pool was now free of weed, my tackle was sound, my rod was an especially lucky one (a 1934 Hardy Victor) and it was surely just a matter of time before I would coax this fabulous creature into my net.

Suddenly, the reel stopped singing and an enormous patch of bubbles broke surface under the far bank. There was a great, bumping swirl and the rod shook and sagged. An amazing dorsal fin rose up, cutting the water from right to left – in the wrong direction – and for the first time I tried to exert some control, winding down and applying as much pressure as I dared. It made no difference at all. But then, not because of anything I was doing, the fish turned and began heading straight towards me, diving majestically into the deep trench that runs along the centre of the pool. I felt it falling,

60

like a sinking liner, and the surrounding trees and hills and clouds were all sucked down after it, snapping back into their rightful positions as the hook sprang free.

I didn't snap back, but went down in the undertow and was lost with all hands.

CHAPTER EIGHT

ISLAMORADA

Neil Patterson

Past dawn: the traffic hadn't started as I crossed US 1 barefoot from the Islander Motel to the breakfast bar. To walk from one side of the key to the other takes one minute twenty. Water birds, so many. A pick-up was parked by the mooring. A trailer paddled at the end of the runway. Behind the jetty I could see the custom vinyl splash rails of a Hewes Bonefisher II lashed to the *Lor E Lei*. Bob had arrived from Plantation, Fort Lauderdale. He must have left as the clubs on the main drag were emptying out.

Almost chilly in the mid-seventies at 7am, but it will be a hundred by noon. I wanted to get across to Channel 5 to Craig Key; to catch the incoming tide. To start a picket line, not join one.

At prime time July, if you're at the end of the line, off the flat in a channel, the tarpon are wary when they get to you. Best to be at the head of the flat. A string is harder to see against the marl, unless they 'daisy chain'; a sort of war dance. Or one comes to the top and rolls. Either way, they're relaxed.

At the end of the queue, there are half a dozen skiffs in front of you. In the sandy channel, you can see the tarpon clearly. They dissolve from the invisible to an oily jet black as they slide off the flat, deep under your feet. They look serene, but they're agitated. They can see you; and they'll see many more like you on their journey to Long Key, Duck Key, Grassy Key; all the way down to Key West, the Marquesas Keys and beyond. Bob was not at ease with my plan.

'We're going somewhere else,' he said.

I thought for a moment. He hung egg on his fork and smiled at my proposal. He was right, of course. He was thinking of being alone; somewhere strategic.

It was too early to be hungry. But after the *Lor E Lei* you can expect nothing aboard *Fly Dipper*. A bottle of water, iced tea from the cooler: no food. I dunked toast in the sweet tar of my coffee. A drip landed like a globule of molten metal on my arm. It had been in full view of yesterday's sun, waiting to raise the rod. It was aching from the tarpon it finally lifted to. The silver king curled in the air, its gills rattling like rubber washers in a can, not six feet from the skiff. It came down in a cloud of shattered crystal, drenching the deck and slamming the rod grip up, badly bruising the underside of my forearm. The streamer failed to find a hold in the Teflon mouth; common enough.

'You wanna fish, let's go,' Bob said as he turned and lowered himself from the bar stool into the eighteen-foot skiff behind, Reeboks the size of canyon runners first. It tipped only slightly.

We might cover a hundred and fifty miles today. At speeds of forty knots, or over. An hour into the ocean, twenty miles into the back country. Maybe across the Gulf of Mexico to Jack's Bank. Avoiding waterspouts or electric storms, the Johnson V4 may only get a chance to cool on the flats for fifteen minute periods.

Out on the ocean, the Hewes was a broadsword, slapping down knee-high waves; making your vertebrae intimate. Poled across a flat, it was a razor blade; slicing through nine inches of glassy water like a length of silk. Not disturbing a grain of sand.

Bob leaned forward, checked the lower unit, pressed the powertilt and started the motor. Birds flew up in their thousands from a small key two hundred yards away. A few roseate spoonbills among them.

The wake washed over Shell Key. Without binoculars, I could see tailing fish. They say this is where flats fishing began. Bonefish up to sixteen pounds have followed the most carefully considered lures. They are rarely taken. A puff of sand made by a Mother of Epoxy lifting from a position in the path of a zig-zagging, mudding bonefish is enough to clear the flat for an hour; maybe two.

A lemon shark patrolled the drop-off. I concentrated on my morning routine. Factor 2 on my face, arms, legs; Factor 4 on my shoulders, chest, stomach; Factor 15 on my ears. English chalkstream fishermen oil their flies. Flats flyrodders oil themselves.

'Go fast. It will cool the air,' I said.

Behind me Bob was standing looking over the glistening surface for 'signs', one hand on the wheel. The leather flaps at the side of his Polaroids kept the sun, and me, from his eyes.

The truth is, there is no shade; nothing can cool you out here. In an hour, the ocean will sing like bare electric wires. The air will crackle like a five bar heater. I could feel the knife in my Dupont shorts warming up like a griddle.

Bob turned on the radio and picked up a Havana station which was playing wild latin music. He tuned to coastal reports and picked up a guide on the CB already staked out on Buchanan Key.

'No wind there, either. Casting won't be dangerous.'

He rubbed Factor 15 into a field of ginger hairs on arms the thickness of my thighs. I thought of all the hooks that must have stuck into him, standing high on the platform behind low-slung, wind-blown back-casts.

'Pierre got a Brown Bunny through his prick,' said Bob, confirming the rumour. 'The fly's framed in the doctor's surgery.'

We followed the markers out past the public ramp at India Key, a cormorant perched on every second one. At 'Bud & Mary's', guides were filling their aerated bait tanks with snapping shrimps. As groundbait, they're effective. Boiled and tossed in mayonnaise, they're delicious. Too good for bonefish, I take them back with me.

Up current from the viaduct, a Columbian family from Miami had a boat anchored and were floating live mullet back towards waiting fish, yelling at Immigration and Federal drug smuggling spotter-planes in Spanish. On the bridge, weekenders promenaded mullet on the surface.

We headed north-east into a heat haze; into the horizon. Thirty minutes later, I wiped fine sea spray off my lenses and saw

Pelican Key. Islamorada was out of sight. Only an electric storm short-circuiting in that direction highlighted the keys.

Bob stopped the engine and took his twenty footer pole up with him onto the platform. He had swapped the foot of his pole for a triangular plastic one since I was last out with him, a year ago. Not many guides use the old guava tree root anymore, cured rock hard in the tropical sun.

We were over three feet of water in a prairie of turtle grass. Bob poled gently in tight circles; like a dog making his bed in a basket. He looked around to check once more, before pushing the pole deep into the marl; screwing, pushing. This was the spot.

This was the place, alright. I looked around for landmarks, clues, markers, 'signs'; anything that could give me a reason why, with nothing on all sides but sea, this was the spot – the pole position. I could see only one thing; Bob's contentment. This, I thought, is what the two hundred and fifty bucks a day buys you. It certainly wasn't lunch.

I looked around, nodding. This was the place. This was the spot they've been passing over since time began. I wasn't going to argue. Not with an age-old fish, fixed in his ways; or Bob, for that matter, even more so.

Roping the skiff to the pole, Bob stepped down and undid the elastic cord on one of the teak rod holders under the gunwale. He handed me a ten-foot Sage and hefty brass SeaMaster charged with a nine floater and three hundred yards of Dacron.

'How far are you expecting these things to run?'

'Cuba.'

I dipped a towel overboard, laid it on the front platform and stepped up. It was dry before I got to it. The bend of a four-inch streamer, with a three-inch orange neck, between the thumb and forefinger of one hand, rod in the other, I balanced precariously; rocking on the balls of my feet.

I watched an egret on a breeze I couldn't feel. For the first time, there was silence. We were alone.

Bob looked for 'signs'. I watched other things. I counted the frigate birds launching from the mangrove nearby. When they're at sea, they can stay aloft for a week. They chase baitfish at sea-level, catching them mid-air as they leap from the surf. Miss, and they drown. They have no oil coating.

We watched for 'nervous' water. Or a 'bust' – an aluminium mouth, like a kitchen bin, sucking at the sun. Tarpon breathe; they have lungs. They come up to the surface, exhale and roll over, refreshed.

'Right, Neil. Get ready.' Bob must have seen one; or some 'signs'. I saw nothing. He poled the boat to ten o'clock.

When a trout fisherman finds himself with the problem of his first tarpon, he adopts a very tense and serious attitude and his reactions are influenced not by what he knows, but by what he thinks he should know; but doesn't. It's a battle between the new knowledge of the sea and the old instinct of the stream.

'Long cast. Nine o'clock. Can you see them? There are four out there.'

Bob poled the skiff round to put me in position. The wind behind, the fish in front. I still couldn't see. My toenails chipped

into the bones of the towel. Then I saw dark shapes. A drip of perspiration bounced down my spine, like a tennis ball.

'Twenty yards. Start casting!' But the rod felt heavy. The line, unfamiliar.

'Go! Too short! Work it! Right, get ready. Now, short cast. Ten o'clock! Not short retrieves! Strip it! Damn it, Neil! Point your rod tip down! Cast again ...'

My line slapped down on the sterling silver skull of the lead tarpon, magic-ing the pod away.

Bob was still hollering at me when the second string suddenly appeared without warning. He saw them the same time I did. But this time my line was aerialised; the back-cast was opening up behind me before Bob had time to part his lips.

The fly landed fifteen yards from the boat, six feet in front of the fish, two feet above a second tarpon lying deeper: one I hadn't seen. It lifted up, up. Out of the flat glare, a platinum salver turned in the sun to engulf my fly. An eye the diameter of a Rolex rolled skywards. Bob had been shouting instructions, but I hadn't heard. My mind was quiet.

'Pump it! Pump it!'

The fly was somewhere inside a potato-peeling machine; sixty yards from the boat, trying to find a hold. The fish was travelling at the same pace at which it intercepted the fly. I pulled once, twice, three times. One for luck.

There was no circus this time. Two hundred yards away by now, I could see the fish swimming with the pod. Bob, skiff, myself, in tow. Bob climbed off the platform and started the engine.

'Why do they do that?' I shouted. He'd already estimated the weight of the tarpon by its length. Nearly five feet. We were attached to a fish the weight of a teenage girl.

Why does such a big fish take such a small fly?'

Bob was watching the parabola mature in my rod. He was calculating the ultimate strength of my leader under load. He was revisiting each knot on my rig, one by one: the Trilene, the Uni-Knot, the Huffnagle, the Bimini Twist.

'Elephants eat peanuts, don't they?'

My eye followed the direction of the tip of the Sage to the high-pitched fuzz where the sea joined the sky. There wasn't a sigh of breeze to shimmer the sheet calm. The only way I knew I was still connected to the fish was by the movement of the boat. The engine silent, the skiff was peacefully heading further out into the ocean; powered by a relative of the herring; a contemporary of the coelacanth. A glint of twisted silver winked at me out of the blue. It reflected in the two corners of my sunglasses.

I pressed the little toothpick into my right side and shifted my body weight onto my left leg; I hung on. A frigate bird lifted off the mangrove as we passed: going fishing. A pelican flapped by the other way; low on the sea, a long way from land: going home.

I looked down at my feet: two chillis. Ahead of me, two hours, maybe three, at the mercy of the migratory whim of one the fourth oldest creatures to still roam the Earth. Somewhere between Man of War and Cluett Keys, I was hitched up to a prehistoric monster, heading for Rabbit Key; wherever that was.

Closing my eyes tight shut, I could feel my heart beating in the bridge of my nose. It was then I realised it had got away. Gazing into blackness; it had escaped, it was free.

I filled my lungs, emptying them in the direction of Cuba.

That 'it' was me.

CHAPTER NINE

NEVER TRUST A POACHER

David Steel

I am very fortunate to have a home and adjoining field which leads down to a hundred-yard stretch of Ettrick Water, one of the tributaries of the Tweed. It used to be good for trout but these have declined over the last twenty years. My particular short beat does not contain any salmon lies. The one deep pool is used by ourselves and most of the village children as a swimming pool in good weather. I don't know if any research has shown that salmon and human habitants don't mix, but anyhow they pass through quickly to the series of deep pools above my part of the river.

One of these – perhaps a mile or so above my house – is at a bend where the river is crossed by an iron bridge leading to a couple of houses and a hotel. It is always fun in clear water to poke your head through the side railings and with Polaroid sunglasses peer into the water directly beneath and count anything up to ten salmon.

We don't get the huge Tweed fish up here – anything from six to nine pounds is the usual. A friend, who owned one of the houses and the fishing, a few years ago gave me and others permission regularly to try our luck in this pool. One afternoon after a poor few hours of trout fishing on a nearby loch I wandered up to take a look, carrying my rod.

I saw a couple of fish, crossed to the other side at the middle of the bend, put a small blue salmon fly on to my trout tackle and determined to have a few casts. I tried over the fish two or three times without success, then thought I would try casting into the rough whirling water at the very top of the pool where a fish might just lie unseen.

On my second cast there I felt a solid resistance unlike the jerking take of a trout. Another snag I thought, but the snag moved! I had indeed hooked a salmon. But I was in trouble, I had light tackle, no waders and was standing awkwardly almost underneath the bridge itself. The fish gave me a tough time rushing up and down the pool and I dared not play it too hard. I saw clearly that it was about seven pounds and my trout cast was of some 4–5 pounds strain. For nearly twenty-five minutes I tussled successfully until I drew the fish into the shallows beside me.

At that point a lad working in the hotel had arrived on the bridge on his motorbike and stopped to admire the fun. All I had was a trout net and I made a couple of unsuccessful lunges at the oversized creature. The lad saw my problem. Would you like me

to come down and land it for you?' I recognised him as one of the expert local poachers. 'Yes please,' was my response. He abandoned his motorbike and clambered down the bank. Sweeping with my net he managed at one go to knock the fish off the hook. With a grateful swish of its tail the salmon disappeared. 'Sorry about that,' he said and got back on his bike. With the benefit of that hindsight which affects all fishermen I realised I should have pulled the fish steadily head first on to the dry shingle and grabbed it by the tail. I would know the next time, but I'm still waiting for that!

CHAPTER TEN

PUTTING YOURSELF ON THE LINE

David Profumo

It has happened to us all, but that hardly makes it any easier: to make contact with a fish, whatever its size, and then to lose it is quite simply sickening. If the loss is unavoidable, then we have to ascribe it to Bad Luck; but if the angler knows that it is a result of his hastiness or incompetence, then he should feel even worse about it.

I like to play my fish hard, and to do this with confidence you must know the limits of your tackle's strength; I am frequently amazed at how many experienced anglers seem ignorant about this. There is much truth in the dictum that trophy fish are caught the night before – when the prudent sportsman will triple-check his gear so that the inevitable impatience of the morrow can be safely indulged. 'One of these days', I remind myself, 'you are going to hook the biggest specimen of your life. Be prepared to land it.'

So much for good intentions. We all know that, despite our best efforts, we are going to lose a percentage of fish we hook – if this were not so, we might as well resort to the speargun. What interests me is the curious way in which these lost fish seem often to gleam more brightly in the memory than those one has actually landed – especially if one has caught sight of them, however briefly.

One famous fishing author with whom I was discussing this volume expressed reservations about a book of stories the outcome of which was known in advance – he felt it stole away all the narrative mystery. Perhaps he has a point: of the four fish I am about to describe, therefore, one of them did not get away, and, though I have a photograph of me proudly holding him, there is a sense in which he is the least memorable of them all.

At the age of fifteen, straggly-haired, acne-hewn and intoxicated with delusions of Hemingway, I was trolling for yellowfins off the coast of Kenya when my rubber Muppet was taken by an enormous shark. The previous day I had landed a Lazy Grey of 118 pounds, but this was something else: this was a creature so large that I could not accommodate it within my current notions of fishiness. He tore nylon off the heavy multiplier and, at what seemed a distance of half a mile or so, juggled his body into the air, twice, like some giant club. I began to pump back line...

When I was twenty, I was lucky enough to be invited for a week to a hallowed stretch of the Restigouche river in New Brunswick, where the fishing was leased by K.C. Irving (of Irving Oil), who had flown in the Royal Flying Corps with my late uncle. As we approached the camp, our helicopter passed over a pool the size of a small lake at the head of which, lying in the thin current, was a grey mass of Atlantic salmon the like of which I have never seen since. At ten o'clock the next morning, my guide anchored our canoe at the top of this pool, and we both peered anxiously downstream.

The sport had been tremendous, and the previous afternoon I had landed fish of 18 and 21 pounds, using the obligatory nine-foot rod and floating line. I felt both tense and confident as we surveyed the many hundreds of salmon now lying below us. There was one in particular which caught our eye, for it was a degree paler in sheen than all the others, and appeared about twice as large: it had taken up a position halfway down the shoal, on the near side. We decided to try for it at once.

Out went the Rusty Rat, swimming for all the world like some little creature in distress, riffling across the stream where the silver runners were stacked. On the fourth cast – against all the odds – our great salmon came off its lie, tipped up its neb, and was hooked. There is not much you can do with a fish clearly over thirty pounds when you are gripping a reservoir rod at the end of which is a length of nylon of twelve-pound breaking strain. It dashed off towards the deeps, then turned and made its way purposefully under the canoe...

Six years ago, I spent a couple of nights at Amhuinnsuidhe Castle in Harris, en route for a week on the fabled Grimersta. For my last morning I was allocated a boat on Loch Voshimid, a tiny water that enjoys the reputation of being the most productive salmon loch in the world.

There was scarcely more than a crinkle on the water – certainly nothing approaching a salmon 'wave' – so I elected to try for seatrout. This is my favourite fish, in any case, and that season had seen a good run.

With just enough breeze to waft out my Grizzled Palmer fly, I was able to practice a little gentle dapping, and rose a couple of finnock on the first drift. In retrospect, I suppose my mind was wandering perilously, my gaze mesmerised by the stumble and pirouette of the fly – I can still see the rise, now, left to right, as the fish took the dap down in a classic porpoise tilt. I waited, murmuring 'God bless the Queen – and her corgis', and tightened. The floss went taut against the cork, and the fish leapt: it looked like a seatrout of well over five pounds, but, as it made off, the floss tore asunder. The next thing I knew, there were some ten yards of pinkish floss lying across the surface, with the fish still attached. I screamed to my boatman to row towards the spot without delay. At least, I think those were my words...

Fishing an autumn week last year on Middle Tweed, we had a high water that was dropping nicely, and there were reports of many fish working their way upstream from the beats below Kelso. There is a powerful cauld pool on this beat, which had not been fishable for a fortnight, but we managed to get the boat up, and I soon had a fish on the fast-sinking line. Then, by casting just beyond the main spine of the current, I put my fly by chance over a large salmon. He snatched it just as it was about to whisk away, and we could see from his back that he was into the twenties. I realised that if we were to have any chance of boating him we would have to get him onto our side of the stream, which was thundering down, and I lugged him towards us before he could settle into his stride.

84

The fish swam up, and then began to circle this unfamiliar side of the pool, no doubt investigating its contours, and he came in close enough on his cruise for us to see him clearly. Although his head was down, and he had hardly begun his fight, I asked the boatman to try a pass at him with the net, if it looked safe...

⋙⋘

The rich tradition of piscatorial literature abounds in tales of loss: some of these accounts are fanciful, others are self-pitying, and many are artlessly overwritten. But the best of them combine a sense of sadness and frustration with a wonder and renewed determination which are surely essential aspects of our pastime. Who can forget the culmination of Bishop G.F. Browne's saga of the fish he lost in 1868 at the confluence of the Tay and Earn – he hooked it just after midday, and at ten-thirty that night, in his own words, 'Up comes the minnow, minus the tail hook. Jimmy rows home without a word; and neither he nor the fisherman will ever get over it.'

These are strong but careful words, from a philosophical divine, but they hardly overstate the case. The loss of a fish – especially if it be a large one, or what a friend of mine has dubbed a 'goliathan' – can haunt you till your dying day. Indeed, in his little poem *The Devout Angler*, Colin Ellis imagines a scene of post-humous redemption for all these traumas wherein St. Peter helps him land Leviathan, hooked on 'celestial gut.' This is a harmless fancy, and there is nothing wrong with a little wishful thinking.

By the same token, I have always thought it was perfectly acceptable to cry over spilt milk. Two major writers have expressed this brilliantly; the sardonic Jonathan Swift, in a letter of 1729, explains 'I remember when I was a little boy, I felt a great fish at the end of my line which I drew up almost on the ground, but it dropt in, and the disappointment vexeth me to this very day, and I believe it was the type of all my future disappointments.' As the fish breaks away, he breaks away a little bit of your heart; and this is one moment of truth among several that angling has to offer.

More recently, in his wonderful book of stories *A River Runs Through It*, the late Norman Maclean reflected on the loss of a huge brownie that had smashed his nylon in a bush, 'Poets talk about "spots of time", but it is really fishermen who experience eternity compressed into a moment. No one can tell what a spot of time is until suddenly the whole world is a fish and the fish is gone,' adding, for good measure – 'I shall remember that son of a bitch for ever.' Maclean was an English Professor for most of his long life, and was not noted for histrionics: all these writers (and one could cite many others) conclude emphatically that they will not forget the experience – ever.

What is going on here, exactly? It has clearly got something more to it than the admittedly regrettable business of a fish getting away, but why all the fuss? I wish I really knew, but I believe it has to do with the intensely personal nature of angling, the probing, exploratory process of casting a lure at an often invisible or, possibly, non-existent quarry. As my cast goes out, I for one imagine I am almost literally putting myself on the line – to the best of my ability, my thoughts go out with the lure to search the water. I am extended, via a fragile umbilicus, into an alien element; my cast becomes a lifeline. Then there is an instant of contact, a glorious, inimitable frisson, a liquid moment that stops the heart and then sends it positively racing – and in this moment, when a great fish flashes as he turns, or the line goes tight, that fish, however briefly, becomes part of the story of that angler's life. Like some lovely girl with whom one has enjoyed a short dance and who is swept away in the arms of a rival, the fish is borne away forever. Small wonder, then, that such irrevocability should arouse lasting passion.

Inexperienced as I was, the shark vaulted one more time, and sheared through the twisted piano-wire trace. He was estimated to weigh more than four hundred pounds. I wore that wire as an amulet around my wrist, until it was lost in the cold mud of the Eton playing-fields; perhaps some archaeologist, centuries from now, will unearth it, and wonder at the presence of a shattered steel trace on the spot where the Battle of Waterloo was held to have been won.

My Canadian salmon passed below the canoe and lunged behind us, wrapping the line around a sunken spruce. We parted company in a trice, and he calmly resumed his position in the shoal. Wilfred Roy, my guide, had been on the river for thirty years, and reckoned it was a fish of over forty pounds.

As the floss began to slide away beneath the surface of the loch, my youthful ghillie 'caught a crab' and fell off his seat. The line snaked with increasing speed down into the nutbrown depths, and we lost our chance of retrieving it. This was my fault, though; I should have checked that the floss had not been frayed from being entangled with flies from my other rod. It was a salutary lesson, and I pray that trout rubbed the hook out before long, and proceeded up the burns to propagate his race.

When my boatman dipped his net, the Tweed fish swam over the rim. He was on the bank, astonished, in less than five minutes, and weighed 28 pounds. He remains my largest salmon, and was one of four I took that morning – a memorable day, by anyone's standards. I have a photograph of him by my desk. I have pictures of those escapees, too. They are only in my head, where they swim through my dreams and remind me of days when it was I that got away – away from the mundane parts of my life, to feel the thrill of a touch on my line, as the life of a fish brushed mine.

CHAPTER ELEVEN

POOL OF THE SUMMER SHIELING

Bruce Sandison

The 'pool of the summer shieling' lies at the heart of the Caithness Flow Country in the far north of Scotland; a remote land, loud with the cry of greenshank, where red deer stalk and otter play. Wild cat hunt wind-burnished moors, golden eagle soar majestically, sleek adders, fat with frogs, laze by russet sphagnum tussocks. Tormentil, bog asphodel, milkwort, sundew and spotted orchid nod in the breeze; wild brown trout stipple the surface, splashing at hapless flies.

A narrow, tortuous road leads out to the loch from Westerdale, past the old grey mill on the banks of the Thurso river, winding across the moor by Loch Meadie and Loch More, into the wilderness. Southwards lie the Caithness mountains: Beinn Glaschoire and Ben Alisky, Scaraben, Maiden Pap, Smean and Morven. To the west, Sletill Hill and the Beinn Griams; and in the distance, the crenellated ridge of Ben Loyal, Queen of Scottish Mountains, and graceful Ben Hope.

91

Mile after mile of these precious moorlands have been devastated by forestry in recent years, but once past Dalnawillan Lodge the landscape is largely unchanged, as it has been for almost six thousand years.

I discovered the loch in the late 1970s, when out in the hills with Roy Eaton, then-editor of the magazine *Trout & Salmon*, and Patrick Sinclair, Lord Thurso's son, who kindly agreed to drive the amphibious Argocat required to transport my illustrious fishing companion across the heather. We had spent the morning on Loch Caol, near Altnabreac, and after lunch headed for Loch Glutt, noted for its crystal clear waters and large, dour trout.

When we arrived at the 'pool of the summer shieling', instead of skirting the lochan, Patrick simply drove straight in and as we drifted across, Roy had a few casts, without success; but I noticed excellent fish rising and stored the information away for future reference.

There are a cluster of waters, the smallest of which dries out during hot summers. They are a delight to fish, regardless of numbers of trout caught, which may generally be counted on the fingers of one hand, given their guile and cunning. Fishing is from the bank but, with care, wading is possible over a large area. Carrying the waders up the hill is another matter, for, in spite of being fairly close to an estate road, on a hot day, the hike over the heather can be soggy and strenuous.

One of the lochs is weed-fringed, barely half an acre in extent, and it is possible to cover much of it with a fly from the shore. The water is dark, the banks soft and squelchy. Indeed, unless otherwise informed, one would pass by without even considering a cast. Which I almost did, and, in retrospect, perhaps should have done; for the memory of my first cast into that peaty darkness still haunts me, as does the sight of the 'one for the glass case' disappearing back into the depths

My wife, Ann, and I had set off early, as much intent on a day's walking as on the removal of trout from their natural habitat. As far as we are concerned, catching fish is of secondary importance; which, given my ability as an angler, is probably just as well.

Eddie McCarthy from the Ulbster Arms Hotel in Halkirk had provided permission, directions and encouragement; the weather was fine for Caithness, and as we parked the car our hopes were high. Golden plovers piped us up the hill as we aimed for the route marker – a grey, broken fence-post, stuck in a hummock. The lochs can't be seen from the track and lie serenely in a shallow hollow on a moorland plateau. It is not until you reach the crest and walk on a few hundred yards that they become visible.

That is why we missed them, in spite of Ann's reasonable warnings. I insisted on bearing too far left and a hot half hour later, on looking back, we found them. As we retraced our steps, I said I was sorry – again.

Proud stags nervously marked our progress. A black-throated diver greeted us, gazing curiously from the middle of the loch, as we settled in the heather by a promontory on the north-east shore. Meadow pipits complained crossly at our intrusion on their privacy. Ann sipped hot coffee. I put up the rods. Standard Sandison procedure. An awesome silence reigned supreme. I scanned the surface of the loch hopefully. Not a sign of a snout anywhere. It was going to be a hard day.

After an hour or so carefully inching round the shores of the main lochs, I decided to walk over and have a look at the little pool to the north. I reasoned that I couldn't do much worse. Two more fish at that stage and I would have caught a brace. I hadn't even seen a trout rise, let alone had an offer. Ann, made of much sterner stuff, fished resolutely on but I suspected that sooner, rather than later, the rod would be abandoned in favour of a sketching pad. I would not be missed.

But anglers are like sheep. The grass on the other side of the fence is always greener. As I surveyed the tiny pool, suspiciously noting the deeply-scarred peat hags overhanging the black water, I instinctively knew that I should hurry back to the principal lochs. Fish were bound to be rising. I should never have left. I was convinced that Ann would have landed at least half-a-dozen and that the day would end, as it frequently did, with me trying, yet again, to say 'Well done!' through fiercely gritted teeth.

On my way over the moor, I had stumbled into a bog and dropped my rod. The 'killer cast', constructed with consummate skill and care, was hopelessly tangled. So, prior to marching, or rather running back, I decided to repair the damage. I was standing at the water's edge, my feet slowly sinking into the marshy ground.

Unhooking the tail fly, a size fourteen Silver Butcher, I reeled off some line and waggled the rod about a bit, half false-casting, in order to give myself some room. The tail fly landed in the water by a clump of weeds and snagged. As flies are designed to do.

Cursing mildly, I tentatively tugged. A huge head appeared from the weeds and lazily grabbed the middle fly, a Soldier Palmer. I stood, speechless, wondering if I was imagining things. Had that really been a trout? Cautiously, I reeled in, tightening. A sail-like tail appeared above the surface, quickly followed by a monstrous, mile-long back. Good grief, it was the most enormous trout that I had ever seen!

My heart raced as I applied pressure. The big trout, lamblike, followed the strain and wallowed towards me. Landing net! Quick, before the trout realises what is happening! I twisted sideways and struggled to free the net. It was stuck fast, cramped between bag and body. Please Lord, I prayed, let the net come free.

I slung the bag viciously round my neck, almost strangling myself, and attacked the net with maniacal fury. By this time my feet were rooted, irreversibly parallel, eighteen inches beneath the bog. The trout waited patiently, tantalizingly close, just out of reach: deep-bodied, gold-spotted, the fish of my dreams.

The net came free and I rocked back and forth, spluttering, lashing it upwards, trying to flick it into a locked position. One arm of the net was caught in the mesh. What had I done to deserve such a fate? I was a good father, a loving husband, helped with the dishes, cut the lawn regularly. Why me? The fish shook its head, vigorously. I froze in terror. Now or never, I vowed.

Reaching forward as far as my trapped position would allow, still cursing the half-open net, I reasoned that if I could manage to get part of the wretched net under the trout, then at least I would have a chance of landing him. Almost there. Another inch. At that moment the trapped arm sprang free and connected with the trout's tail. I staggered back, sinking into wet slime.

The water exploded as the trout decided that enough was enough. Spray sparkled and the weeds parted. Back and tail clear of the surface, he turned and ran for the middle. My snagged Silver Butcher pulled free. The rod was almost wrenched from my hands as the reel screamed in anger. I hung on, watching helplessly.

Leaving a wake like the Queen Mary, the huge fish steamed across the loch. It gave one mighty, spectacular leap, and my cast broke. Waves rippled through the reeds by my feet. A lark sang, derisively. I slumped on the moor, wet, muddy, stunned and utterly dejected.

Collecting together what remained of my broken tackle and spirits, I trudged miserably over the heather to Ann. Who would believe me? Would I ever see the like again? I was greeted with a cheery wave and the sight of a brace of beautiful trout: 'There, I told you. Perseverance, that's all it takes. How did you get on?' Through mist-filled eyes, I managed to gasp: 'Not bad. Had an offer, a huge trout, but it got away.' I poured out my tale of woe.

Ann smiled knowingly: 'Yes, dear, I've heard it all before. Another one of your tall stories about "the one that got away". Stop brooding. Time for home. Come back another day. He'll still be there.' As we trailed down the hill in the evening sunlight, I knew that I'd never go back. Nor have I. It wouldn't be right.

CHAPTER TWELVE

THE TROUT THAT SAID THANK YOU

Conrad Voss Bark

t's a very strange thing, the brain. There are certain things it hangs on to and can reproduce again and again as small colour pictures inside itself. You can see these quite clearly, small colour television pictures inside your head, that are vivid and detailed towards the centre and blurred towards the outside of the frame, just as you saw them ten, twenty, thirty or even fifty years ago.

There are times when I can still see quite vividly a schoolboy hopping around the hockey pitch hanging on to his shin in one hand, which had been hit, shouting 'play on, play on' to the rest of us not to stop the game for an injury. This was an incident which must have happened some fifty or fifty-five years ago and yet I can still see it quite clearly in the television set in my head.

Why do such things happen? I do not know. The schoolboy incident had no particular significance. It was slightly comic, I suppose, but that was all. More important things that have happened are often not capable of recall. Why does the video in your head pick out something or other and keep it there for years and years, ready to be played whenever you want to see it again? Sometimes of course these brain pictures are significant as was the case with the trout that said 'thank you'.

This is how I think of it. It was how I thought of it at the time and so, when I recall the picture, that is how I still think of it. It was all very odd and I will try to tell it as accurately as I can, which is not all that easy as any eye-witness will tell you.

It was about eight or ten years ago. I was fishing for trout on the river Lyd which runs near my home in Devon. This is a very beautiful river that rises on Dartmoor and comes down the valleys into pastoral country and sweeps past our house with a great swirl and chuckle of water over the stones. There is one part of the river a little further up from our house where it takes almost a right-angle bend. It is quite shallow and often I have passed it by but on this particular day at the far corner of the bend there were one or two large stones and a gurgle of water going over them and just behind the stones I had a guess might be a fish. I was fishing a dry fly – these Devon streams are wonderful dry fly water – and I cast it above the stones in the smooth run knowing pretty well that by the time the fly was turned over and over in the turmoil behind the stones it would probably be a wet fly or, as Horace Brown of the Piscatorials once said, it would be slightly damp.

So it was. I did not see the take but I saw the line hesitate in the flow and begin to belly downstream and tighten and there was the fish, a very good fish indeed for our water, for we pride ourselves on our wild brown trout, most of them small but wonderful fighting fish that never give up. They are as furious as fresh-run seatrout and so was this because it was large for the Lyd, maybe a pound, maybe more, and eventually it came in.

It was tired and not fighting as it held itself up in the shallows by my feet, and you could see how tired it was, but when I got a full view of it I was entranced by the colours of the body. In our rivers you get brown trout which are not brown at all but a glorious mixture of the most vivid colours imaginable, carmine spots, a silvery green back, a bright butter-yellow belly, and everything matched together and startlingly vivid like a pointilliste painting. It was so beautiful that I suddenly felt I couldn't kill it. It was too beautiful.

So I slid my fingers down the leader until I could get hold of the shank of the hook which was projecting from the left side of the fish's mouth. I can remember that very distinctly. Before fishing I had pressed down the barb so that if I caught a salmon parr it could be released without damage. Most of us now fish barbless for that reason. So in this case – and the trout was not struggling – a sudden push down of the hook and it came away. Now it happened.

The fish could certainly feel the pluck as the hook came away for its head had moved with the pressure, and therefore it was aware of freedom. It allowed the current to move it slightly sideways until it was about a foot or just more than a foot away from my fingers which were still in the water. I'd had to bend down and did not

103

immediately remove my hand so most of it was still under water. At that moment – and it all happened very quickly – the fish stopped, turned, and came back towards my fingers and looked at them, or at least that is was it appeared to do. It stayed looking at my fingers – it was about nine inches or so away from them – for a moment, maybe a second, two seconds, no more, and then slid away faster than before into the current and was gone. I was left crouching, my hand still in the water, looking after the fish until it disappeared.

And my brain video is of the fish looking at my fingers in this most curious way. about nine inches or so from my fingers, a vivid picture in full colour, hazy at the edges but the fish's face and my fingers remarkably clear. What on earth, I thought to myself at the time, what on earth did it think it was doing, coming back like that?

I have had several explanations offered, and some may be true, and nothing to do with a fish's emotion or feelings, and it may well be that a tired fish may be confused and bewildered by what has happened and does not quite know what to do and where to go. Yes, I think that may be so, but personally I have a hankering after the original impression I had which was that the fish was coming back to examine these strange pink things which had suddenly taken out the nasty thing in its mouth and given it back its freedom. Was it thankful? Was it expressing gratitude? I do not know. But every time I recall that video in my brain and look at it I am still inclined to think there is some emotion there in that lovely fish that could possibly be interpreted as gratitude. Absurd, of course, but entirely impossible? I leave it to you.

CHAPTER THIRTEEN

OVER THE VOLCANO

Bernard Venables

his is a story that perhaps has no rightful place in this book. Its subject – not salmon, nor trout, nor great amber carp – is a whale: no fish at all but a huge sea-haunting mammal. If indeed its story is justified here it is because in its essence there is no difference. The angler's link with his quarry has no parallel among field sports; it has a poignancy that is half love. So it is with this story, but on a scale so epic as almost to touch high tragedy.

It is an improbable story. How can the second half of the twentieth century contain so strange a survival; how can it be that men still engage so primevally with nature? In the Azores, lost in the oceanic vastness of the Atlantic, men go in small open boats to pit themselves against this marine monster – a bull sperm whale whose length may be 65 feet. To this dire engagement they go with weapons pygmy for so great a quarry: nothing but hand harpoons and hand lances. Not for them the easy slaughter obscenely wreaked from the safety of a factory ship. Their encounters, day by day, echo the stark frame that has been nature's since the time of the dinosaurs – the predatory balancing of species against species for the best equity of life on earth. These are gentle men: they harm nothing but the sperm whale; the sperm whale harms nothing but the giant squid which is its prey; the giant squid harms nothing but that which gives it its subsistence.

Necessity impels these Azoreans. They are pitifully poor; they must face fearful dangers for the minuscule rewards which whaling wins. But these are also men of a peculiar aptitude. Their nature is that of their islands – outwardly serene, but beneath the surface a volcano simmers. They are kindly men, child-loving, but with a smouldering passion which the perils of whaling ignite. Such is the danger that any day may see a whale, pitifully pestered by its hunters, rise in vast ferocity, smashing the boat, killing the men. Any day's return from sea is met by wives and children with entwining arms, grateful for one more safe return.

Of those days which I shared with these whalers, this is the story of one.

As the first light of dawn dimmed the stars I was at Castelo Branca. Under the fall of land, between fangs of volcanic rock, there lay two whale boats, 37 feet long. They are called canoas (pronounced 'canooa'); they lie ready for the instant's bidding. In the bows there is a cross-plank called a 'clumsy cleat', or thigh board, which has a semi-circular notch to take the bracing of the harpooner's thigh. Before him in the bow's peak are the chocks, a cleft to take the running of the whale line. In readiness beside the thigh board are harpoons and lances. Further back are the thwarts and the mast ready for stepping and in the stern the 'cuddy board'; on that stands the loggerhead, a bollard tapered outward from its base. As an angler plays his fish by line and reel, so the boatheader plays a whale by the giving and taking of line round the loggerhead. On either side below the cuddy board are the standing cleats – straddled on these, the boatheader stands for vision ahead. So standing he can use either the rudder or the 22-foot steering oar – rudder under sail, steering oar when going with oars.

Now we wait, the seven crewmen of the boat and I; we wait for the knell which is to send us to whatever is to be the fate of this day. Here is José Fula, the boatheader of our canoa; Antonio Fula the harpooner, and there are five others, one of them a boy in his mid-teens for whom this is his first trial day. We wait for the lookouts. They, with binoculars, on high vantages round the island of Fayal, have overlapping arcs of vision. So from first light they scan the ocean distances for the blowing of a whale. When sighted, it may be thirty or more miles offshore. We are waiting with such stoicism as we can muster for the signal-rocket which shall rouse us into action.

Across the five-mile strait is the perfect volcanic cone of the island of Pico. In this pallid pause between dawn and sunrise all is held in a sense of unreality. The sea lies quiet; the faint swell catches the light like slashed lead. Minutes accumulate.

An effulgence fans up behind Pico, strengthens, floods up the sky. The rising of the sun releases our worst tension; still we wait.

Five o'clock comes and passes, then six o'clock; a little past seven the hush is shattered; a rocket is rising, hissing, rising interminably; it bursts, resounds from the heights and we are running to the boats. Then we are afloat, paddling out to the two tow launches just offshore. This day I am going on the tow launch, not in a canoe as on other days. I go aboard and we take our canoas in tow. The launches' throttles roar, our wakes fold white on the ultramarine sea. The little harbour falls astern. With the east's molten blaze behind us we go arrow-straight due west to where, many miles beyond our seeing, a whale is blowing.

Under Fayal's precipitous plunge to the sea we surge on, the canoas bucketing in our wakes. The men, crowded aft, are silhouettes against the eastern light. At the fall of the first hour we pass under Capelhinos, then the raw red cone of the new volcano is on our beam, soon falling back under the starboard quarter. Now we are taken by the vast blue anonymity of sea and sky.

Fayal drops astern, its craggy heights melt to gossamer; Pico dissolves into the dazzle over the stern. Then both are gone and nothing breaks the horizon's infinite rim.

After four hours, sentiently there is a change; the men stir. A current, part instinct, part experience, possesses them. On each launch a man swarms to masthead. The launches veer apart, casting about. Then from our canoa, *Sao Jaoa Baptista*, there is a cry: 'Bloz', they shout and point over our starboard bow. About a mile away, over the swell's recession there – there it is – a stubby, vaporous cloud, mushroom-coloured – the blow of a sperm whale.

We stop; the canoa casts its tow; we roll in the huge silence.

Sao Jaoa Baptista is stepping its mast, raising sail; the sail hesitates, fills with a slap loud in the silence. The whale blows and blows, idling, secure in its ocean loneliness. Now the men have taken to the paddles and sit on the gunwales facing forward, digging in rapid rhythm. The canoa lifts, almost skims. José at the tiller is on the standing cleats; Antonio, heavy-shouldered at the thigh board, hangs loose arms until the climactic moment shall claim him. Still the whale moves in its slow peace 'having its spoutings out', serene and monstrous in the sun.

The canoa is closing on the whale; seconds pass compressed with fearful elation. Antonio picks up the harpoon, raises it rigidly poised, bracing into the thigh board. Still the whale dallies in its innocence in the sun; it blows with the sound of surf receding over shingle.

José is taking the canoa to the whale *cabeca con cabeca* – head to head – the way of greatest danger, straight towards the great bluff of its head, within the very narrow zone of no forward vision. At the very last second he lays his weight to the steering oar, turning the canoa round the head, into vision, and in towards the body behind the head, judging with such exquisite fineness that it is the boat that lives, not the whale. Antonio doubles in a plunging thrust. The harpoon is in. The whale is fastened.

In a blinding smother the stricken whale throws up mighty flukes, then sounds; line tumbles through the chocks. In the bouncing seethe, stays and halyards are let go, the mast and bundled mainsail let down to lie over the quarter. The plunging line wrenches down the bows, taking water. A hundred fathoms pour away, then two hundred; the whale levels off, slows. José makes a first attempt to snub the line at the loggerhead; the bows wrench down taking on water again. The whale sounds more deeply, runs again.

Now the burning torrent of line slackens, hesitates, wrenches spasmodically. The men stand, straddling the thwarts; they haul, gain line yard by yard by drag of muscle, José coiling it down with exactitude so that no flake shall foul another for fear of disaster. He tempts opportunity to snub it again at the loggerhead, this time holding it. The bow plunges; the shivering canoa in headlong tow runs as if powered, bows sheering the sea. Water is poured on the smoking line lest it take fire at the loggerhead. Now the first frenzy is abating. The line slackens; the whale is lifting.

The sea itself bursts open; a grey enormity of whale wallows, thrashing with flippers and flukes, blowing. The flukes are flung up, the whale rounds out and sounds. But it sounds less deeply; fury so frantic is taking its toll. But still it runs, burning away the tumbling line. It slackens, the whale rises; the men astride the thwarts once more gain line. José snubs it at the loggerhead. The whale is running erratically now in a wild staccato. José gains a few turns at the loggerhead, loses them, gains them again. The relentless line is wearing down the mighty strength, nagging it into weakness. The whale arcs about the boat's axis; beating the sea in pestered confusion. Now the men, standing, take the line in the bow cleat for 'bowing' on the whale, edging in towards its quarter. Antonio at the thigh board waits with a heavy droop of shoulders.

Foot by foot the canoa closes in. Now it is very near; the huge, hurt beast beats the sea. Now is the time of greatest danger:

one touch of the enormous flipper would smash the boat.

Now – a pause deadly quiescent – the boat goes in from aft towards the flipper. Antonio is poised with the lance. The canoa touches the whale – wood on black skin. In a second, Antonio's throttled waiting bursts through thighs, buttocks, plunging arms. His lance enters to its shaft. The whale rolls in anguish, flippers and flukes lashing. It seeks to sound, plunges, surfaces, all in awful proximity to the boat's fragility. The oars back water several strokes, Antonio strains on the lance warp for the sucking free of the lance. The whale turns sub-surface and runs beneath the boat, lifting it teetering. Staggering, weaving, the giant once again rises, thrashing the swell. The surf is pink.

Now the canoa, like a predatory animal poised for pouncing, waits on opportunity. It comes during a quiet pause; the canoa goes in. Antonio from two fathoms off lobs his lance. It seems to hang, arrested, then drops, penetrating all the length of its wrought iron shaft. Slowly, beating, the whale rolls and blows. The blow is also pink.

On the canoa, a red waif is hoisted; at its bidding we on the launch close in. The whale labours inconsequentially. The sea is reddening. The canoa closes, lances again. The whale blows; the blow is opaque now – a gout of blood; sighing blow after blow drenches the sea. In dreadful sequence the boat comes in again and again.

Now the whale has lost all purpose; it rolls awash, moving in shuddering spasms. Once it lifts its flukes, slapping them explosively. It is in 'the flurry'; the end is imminent. We wait.

113

Suddenly resurgent life bursts upon the whale; an enormous convulsive lunge throws it up, half out of the sea. Its flukes are spread out. Then it sounds. The line empties away, vertically – a hundred fathoms, two hundred, and thirty more. At last it stops. No movement now. The line is a vertical iron rod. The whale has dived to die. Apart from rare exceptions, a whale dies at the surface.

Now what depth of stoicism must be summoned? A quarter of a mile beneath the surface lies that immense body. How are seven men to lift it? But the men sit placidly on the thwarts; they smoke, they talk quietly. What shall come shall come.

We wait in the vast blue peace of the ocean; a balm of silence lies upon us. *Sao Jaoa Baptista* is held a little down at the bows by its remote anchorage. So we must wait until help summoned by radio shall come. I lie drowsing on the foredeck of the launch. Time passes beyond conjecture.

Then two bow waves, remote dots, appear out of the haze that is Fayal. They grow to become a tuna boat and a launch towing a canoa. From the canoa go its seven men, from the tuna boat two more, into *Sao Jaoa Baptista* – sixteen men in a craft designed for seven. To the raw wet line they set their hands. In the bows Antonio chants softly to set a rhythm. They begin to haul, foot by foot.

Time passes; Antonio sings. The hauling becomes hypnotic – unless made mindless how could there be faith in an end? They draw six inches at each haul; their hands bleed. One man puts his socks on his hands. Five hours pass; then at last, through the clear water, the whale can be seen, a vague shimmer of a shape, perhaps thirty fathoms down. But how can it be raised from that last depth, horizontally, not vertically, so that a tow warp can be put to its tail?

It is rare for a whale to die this way. By chance we have with us Bruno Vailati who by aqualung diving is here to film whaling below and above surface. He puts on his suit, takes a rope and dives. Now the suspense is drum-taut. We scan for sharks. At last he surfaces; he has bent the rope round the peduncle of the whale's tail.

Now we all haul, sixteen in the canoa, and we on the launch. The harsh line bites at our hands and muscles burn to the limit of bearing. But, at last, it is done. The great grey island of body is awash on the surface. Now with the towing strap about the peduncle, the towing warp is bent to it. The two launches, in line, take the whale in tow. At only two knots it will take all night to gain back those many miles to shore and the whale factory.

Exhausted and grateful, we board the tuna boat. In the dark, five hours later, we drag ourselves from the deck to the harbour quay.

It is morning when we hear that half a mile offshore the tow lost its hold, that the whale had sunk, was lost. Tragically, it was one that got away. For nothing had that pitiful ocean giant lost its life. For nothing had the men endured and faced appalling danger. If the whale is not brought to the factory they receive no money.

CHAPTER FOURTEEN

GOING FOR BUST

Chips Keswick

The size of a fish may not be important to the true angler but, if one is honest, a large fish promotes an excitement which clouds one's judgement and makes one do things which a smaller prize would not. I should add that I started fishing aged six in a Scottish burn with a worm and have fished with passion all over the world ever since.

In 1966 I went to fish the Sunndal river in Norway. The beat belonged to a famous English fisherman, Harry Bridgeman, who personally caught over a thousand salmon there in a lifetime's fishing. I travelled by air to Oslo, caught the sleeper train to Oppdal and then took the local bus some twenty miles down the river to the Edwardian lodge used by people fishing the beat. The lodge had a corrugated iron roof, clapboard walls and an outside privy with no door. Wild strawberries grew in profusion on the privy roof and you went about your obligations with a beautiful view of a good pool one hundred feet below. This part of day took some time due to the strawberries and the utter tranquillity of the surroundings. The lodge had iron bedsteads with sagging frames, and to lie in one was like sleeping in a hammock. The prevailing memory, as usual, was the smell: a charming combination of local cheese, salami and bottled beer which were the staple ingredients of all the meals including breakfast. There was also a general feeling of pervading damp.

The routine was identical every day – breakfast at eight, a visit to the strawberry-covered privy, greasing or ungreasing the green Kingfisher lines according to the air temperature and onto the river by 11am. We fished with sixteen-foot greenheart rods, 50 lb breaking-strain nylon and yards of backing on old Hardy fly reels of a kind now much sought-after by collectors. Our waders were made of stitched canvas with outside boots and socks over the canvas to prevent wear at the ankle. We had no car so we walked or bicycled to the river with our rods carried backwards over our shoulders.

The beat we fished had six pools spread over four miles with one very dubious suspension bridge in the middle to cross over. If you suffered from vertigo this was a major hazard since it was slung some fifty feet above a massive set of rapids strewn with large boulders. The river at this point was some sixty yards across. It really was not a place for the faint-hearted.

By any standards the Sunndal was – and no doubt still is – a big braggart of a river, unforgiving to the careless wader or the greedy striver of an extra yard in order to cover all the water. I never went home dry and I now doubt, in middle age, if I would take

the same risks I took 25 years ago. The river was best in early June, not very prolific but with big fish, seldom less than fifteen pounds and often over thirty. On average you landed one a day and lost two or three due to incompetence, breaks or the massive power of the river which rose a foot most days by 3pm when the snow in the mountains melted in the summer sun. It never got dark and the best fishing was when the river started to drop in the cool of the evening about 10pm. Then we fished until we were exhausted at about 1am.

My most painful memory from that marvellous river is of a large salmon – well over 30 lb – which I hooked from a boat while flyfishing. I had with me an old Norwegian gillie rowing the boat and as it was a wild day he wore an old tin bucket on his head – with good reason for we went down the pool pinging like a church clock when I struck him with the fly on the forward stroke.

I caught a 17 lb fish, which threatened to leave the pool but was persuaded otherwise by my allowing the line to go slack, and we then worked the fish back into the pool by leaving the reel alone and rowing the boat upstream, leading the fish as if it were a dog.

We started down the pool again and the largest salmon I have ever hooked took the fly and set off back to the sea. On this occasion however, because of its size, I failed to repeat the prudence I had shown with its smaller companion and fought it all the way to the tail of the pool and the ensuing rapids. I ended up losing my entire line and backing which snapped at the join to the drum.

I have regretted my heart ruling my head ever since.

CHAPTER FIFTEEN

PLAYING THE APRIL FOOL

George Melly

I t is the first of April, and a boisterous if fitful wind is howling round my attic room in Scethrog Tower, a Norman building, originally intended to repel the Welsh, but converted into a farmhouse in the sixteenth century.

By turning my head to the left I can see, through the oak mullioned window in the three-foot wall, and within a few hundred yards across an uneven lush green field, a silver-grey elbow of the River Usk where I own almost a mile of horse-shoed bank. It is here, under the steep hills, that I do most of my fishing.

I've been out all morning, casting between gusts and with nothing to show for it. There was very little fly and I only saw two fish move in three hours, one rise apiece. I got over them alright but they weren't interested in either a March Brown or a Dark Olive. Tomorrow however, or even this afternoon if the wind drops, I'll be out again. Optimism, renewed at every cast, reborn each day, is

123

essential to the committed angler; an indication of mild lunacy for those to whom the whole process is inexplicable.

The Usk is like a wayward, unpredictable mistress with nothing in common with the domestic virtues of the famous southern chalkstreams where I have occasionally been privileged to fish.

There are no mowed banks or gently swaying weeds, no little benches for the comfort of the retired military or elderly members of the judiciary. Access to some of the best pools is under the electric fence and, in summer at any rate, through chest-high barriers of nettles and malicious brambles. Wading is essential and occasionally treacherous. The winter spates can alter the whole geography of the bottom, excavating deep pools where before there was an even shelf of sand or pebbles. Strong currents materialise in high water like insistent sirens.

The Usk, after heavy rain, can rise with alarming speed. It can flood the surrounding fields, subsiding again equally abruptly, and occasionally stranding migrating salmon, their eyes soon to be pecked out by crows and magpies. Conversely, in a drought, it can dwindle to a meandering trickle reducing the evening rise to a tense and frustrating five minutes.

I love its unpredictable nature, and of course it can be benign; its waters slightly coloured and at the right height, the air warm, the trout rising along its whole length.

And what trout! They are all wild, and ferocious fighters. Their flesh is as pink as a sewin, every shade from palest rose to deep red. Their average weight is just over a pound but to hook one is to engage a creature bearing little in common with the sluggish rainbows of the put-and-take reservoirs or even the pampered stock fish of the Avon, Itchen, Test, or Kennet. Not that I'm against fishing these waters. On the contrary, when the capricious trout of the Usk decide to with-hold their favours, it is essential for my *amour-propre* to go elsewhere; to prove it is not just me who is responsible for an empty creel; that trout are susceptible, can be deceived, will take. Nevertheless there is no moment I treasure more than returning at dusk with a brace of fish caught on my own water. My ebullient air of triumph is inexplicable to my non-angling family, and must be repressed if I am to avoid ridicule.

I have mentioned salmon but they are mostly late autumn transients when my profession compels me to be elsewhere. I have only killed one and lost another in the fifteen years I've been here despite a formidable number of devons and spoons embedded in under-water hazards; enough to stock a small shop. There are occasional shoals of seatrout too; exhilarating provokers of adrenaline; more often lost than landed with their soft mouths and violent knocks. It is, however, trout that I go for. Trout which take so often in my dreams, and sometimes in reality.

I have already given the average weight of those fish taken as just over a pound, but there are of course much bigger ones, much bigger, that rise on summer evenings when the air is thick with flies, and usually in inaccessible stretches. The heaviest I've actually grassed was just under three pounds, caught on a dry fly on my birthday some years ago and on practically my last cast before I had to go and pack to return to London. I've had bigger fish on, occasionally, but never for long enough to see them and usually in high water so that they may well have been sewin or small salmon. But there is a trout which I've hooked three times, and seen, and I would guess conservatively that he weighs at least five pounds. He appears to have a malicious sense of humour. Nor is it just I who have hooked this triton. When I am on tour the fishing is often let, and reading last year's entries at the beginning of this season, I came upon this account: 'Dick Atkins lost good fish on underwater hazard in Molly's Gutter...'

Well, Dick Atkins is not alone there. The 'good fish' which lives under the far bank of the Mink Island pool is, I'm sure, my elusive escapologist. He takes deceptively mildly and appears well-hooked. He gives at first, swimming towards me with very little resistance and then, almost as I reach for the net, turns and bends the rod double as he zooms back across the pool and the reel screams in anguish – surely the most exciting sound in the world.

Twice on our encounters he's leapt into the air, an awe-inspiring sight honoured by my rod. He seems to tire, but only briefly. At a moment chosen by him, having ignored this obvious refuge until he judges the timing will create the maximum disappointment, he takes off again, turns along the side of Molly's Gutter – a narrow, very deep holding pool where I hooked my lost salmon – and bores down to wrap the cast around a submerged tree just visible far below the surface in very low water, and makes his escape. I suppose I could have this tree removed with grapples, blocks and a tractor, but I shan't. If I ever beat him it must be fair and square, and on a light tackle, four pounds breaking point at most, and then, one April noon or August evening...

Quite recently, I read an article claiming the notion of the 'educated' trout to be a myth, that the trout's brain was too small to accommodate a learning programme, that it was a pure machine, that 'the one that got away' does so because it is heavier and stronger. I am aware too that my account is absurdly anthropomorphic. I'm sure my trout is eager to escape from the moment it is hooked. None the less its repetitive behaviour is puzzling and provocative. It is impossible to rid myself of the undoubted illusion that I am not playing it. The fish is playing me.

CHAPTER SIXTEEN

ONE THAT SHOULD HAVE GOT AWAY

Jeremy Paxman

Imagine, if you can, Harrogate transported to the tropics. The Sri Lankan coastal plain, doubly deluged by biannual monsoons, swelters through most of the year. But up in the central highlands, it is forever England. Oil-green tea plantations run over the hillsides as far as the eye can see, splashed here and there by the brightly-coloured saris of the tea pickers.

Then, suddenly, you are in mock-Tudor gentility. A half-timbered general store, the ochre sign 'Cargill's' fading in the sunlight, stands on one corner, across the road the paint is peeling from the Victorian racecourse grandstand. In the midst of this gutta-percha Godalming stands the Nuwara Eliya Hill Club, four-square respectability behind rose beds and close-mown lawns.

131

The Hill Club was the place to which the colonial British retreated when the heat and the humidity all got too much, the memsahibs had been packed off on returning P&O steamers and teaplanters and administrators felt the need for few evenings of Rangoon Billiards in the misty chill of the highlands. We arrived there in time for dinner (mulligatawny soup, roast beef and spotted dick, ties of varying age supplied to those who thought they didn't need them on holiday).

Before retiring to the roaring fire in the bedroom, I asked the club secretary where on earth the several five or six pound trout in glass cases around the hall had come from. 'From Horton Plains, sir,' he answered, in that incredulous tone of voice which makes you feel half educated. They were marvellous, full-bellied and deeply stippled specimens. Could a day's fishing be had?

Indeed it could, the keeper would be here at seven next morning with the landrover.

Mr Cruz, a stocky chap in an out-the-elbows cardigan was there on the dot, and he didn't come alone. There was his staff too: a short, perpetually smiling man who would drive us up to the plains, and a gaunt and gloomy fellow dressed in an ankle-length black oilskin and wearing a massive black sou'wester on his head. He was from the government fisheries department, said the keeper. He looked more like a representative of the local undertakers.

Mr Cruz, the smiling driver, Mephistopheles and I set off for Horton Plains, making slow progress as we stopped on one bend or another to lift a fallen tree off the road (Mephistopheles remained in lugubrious immobility on these occasions; beneath his dignity, I imagine). Finally, we reached the plains. Anything more different from the steamy rainforests below would have been hard to imagine. They were cold, bleak, wet and windswept, not unlike the Cheviots on a blustery November afternoon.

It was now that Mr Cruz produced his tackle. There was, first, the net: a small, fine-gauged implement, a bit like the sort of thing children use on rock-pool expeditions. It was lashed together with string and old bits of nylon, but it would do the trick if we ever caught anything.

Which, from the state of the rest of the tackle, looked questionable. The rod was fibreglass, about nine feet long, and also held together with bits of twine, nylon and tape. The line, an old greased line which had lost its coating and its grease, was attached by a yard or so of rather heavy-looking nylon to a single fly of no known pattern. It too had seen better days, so that all that was left was one brown wing, a little tinsel on the body, and the remnants of a yellow tail. It was, said Mr Cruz, the only fly he had. Mephistopheles gave us a cold glare, and off our little army marched across the plain towards the stream.

In the mid-nineteenth century, Sir Samuel Baker used to hunt elk-hounds across Horton Plains, but the trout fishing wasn't developed until the 1880s, when a tea-planter raised twenty brown trout from ova shipped out from England and discovered they could grow prodigiously in the Ceylon streams. Until then, it had been thought that trout couldn't survive south of the 24th parallel, but within fifteen years, specimens of 7¾lbs, 8¼lbs, and one of 9lbs – taken while being pursued around a pool by an otter – had been caught. Rainbow fry imported from New Zealand did even better, and were soon breeding – and eating – furiously. One angler in 1909 noticed an abnormal swelling on the belly of a 5 lbs rainbow he'd caught, cut the fish open and discovered part of the udder of a cow and one teat.

The water too appeared promising, rich and peaty-looking. There were all the usual characteristics of a British trout stream, fast little narrows and broader pools, although with little or no cover. Our expeditionary force halted at the riverbank and watched. Nothing. Not the faintest suggestion of a hatch of fly or a rise. Mr Cruz handed me the rod and I cast away for an hour or so, dibbling the fly down through the runs and working it in the necks of the pools. The stream looked as if it ought to be full of fish, the record book and the glass cases suggested it was, but there still wasn't the slightest sign of life.

We moved on down. Golgotha pool commemorated the spot, said Mr Cruz, where a party of pilgrims had been murdered. For years afterwards, anglers could look down and see their skulls grinning up from the bottom. Mephistopheles' kind of place.

For another couple of hours I worked the water with the single fly, but we saw nothing and felt nothing, and it looked absolutely certain that this would be the day they all got away. We stopped to eat the great doorsteps of sandwiches cut for us by the Hill Club. And then it started to rain. Great, solid sheets of it, pouring down like stair-rods. For the first time, the flicker of a smile crossed Mephistopheles' face beneath his vast sou'wester: the rest of us had no waterproofs.

'Mr Cruz,' I said, 'I think it's time for us to reconsider.'

'To tell the truth, sir,' he said, 'they don't like to come to the fly very often.'

It looked the sort of stream which should be full of good-sized trout, but was probably also full of all manner of good food on the bottom. We could try a different pattern, I thought for a moment, then remembered we had no other pattern. Then, Mr Cruz had an idea.

'Sir,' he said, sensing my predicament and his opportunity, 'what you need are these.'

He reached into his right-hand trouser pocket and drew forth a palm full of writhing fat worms. If he'd produced a wriggling white rabbit, I would not have been more surprised. He looked at the worms and then at me.

'But Mr Cruz,' I said, 'according to the rules, this is fly-only.'

'It's alright sir. When all else fails...'

Here was a real ethical dilemma. Mephistopheles, the man from the ministry, ought to know whether the use of worms was acceptable, but he looked smugly inscrutable through the rain. I was cold, wet and on the point of giving up, anyway. I succumbed.

We used the fly to attach one of the plumpest worms to the cast, and I trotted it down the stream. Within two minutes there was a take, and two or three minutes after that, a perfect fat trout had come to the net. Mr Cruz knocked it smartly on the head and laid it on the bank.

I ought, I suppose, to have felt triumphant, and in a way I did. It was a beautiful, richly marked rainbow of about a pound and a half. True, I had taken it on a worm, but it wasn't as if I'd speared it, or thrown a stick of dynamite into the water.

But when he caught my eye, Mephistopheles seemed to read my mind. He knew it ought to have got away.

CHAPTER SEVENTEEN

THE MONSTER OF CLAPHAM BECK

Laurence Catlow

In fifty years of fishing there have been many lost trout; almost all of them have brought a sense of something like bereavement. Sometimes the hurt has soon healed, chased away by bigger and better trout that have stayed for the net; sometimes the day has already brought trout enough, so that the loss of one more has seemed only a small sorrow. And sometimes I have been untypically resilient, able to absorb and overcome failure, while at other times my mood has been more vulnerable, which means that losing a trout brings a pain that stays. But there is one lost trout that is unlike all those other lost trout: a trout that has haunted my dreams for more than forty years.

My brief encounter with him came during the second of three undergraduate summers, three long summer vacations that were devoted almost exclusively to fishing, three summers when, from June to the end of September, I spent four or five days a week on the headwaters of the Wenning in North Yorkshire, where the bold form of Ingleborough looked down on my still-clumsy attempts to catch trout on the dry fly.

It was a lovely stretch of water. There was about a mile of the river, a limestone river winding its way through rough and lonely pastures; above this there were the becks that made the Wenning: Fen Beck, Austwick Beck and Clapham Beck. There were salmon and sea trout in the pools and the water swarmed with parr, but I went to the Wenning and her becks in search, not of fish from the sea, but of stay-at-home brown trout. Throughout my fishing life it is the spotted beauty of brown trout that has drawn me to rivers; it is the way of a brown trout with a fisherman's fly that has fascinated, frustrated and fulfilled me, sending me home sometimes in profound dejection, but sometimes full of a joy too intense and too unqualified for a creature aware of his own mortality. The day at the heart of this story ended in bitter despondency, and yet it was a day that had brought me to the Wenning in a mood of high festival.

It was a day late in August and the morning post had brought my examination results, which were all that I had dared hope for: a source of deep relief and much deeper satisfaction because academic success was very important to me, every bit as important, in fact, as catching trout. Of course that day late in August was immediately proclaimed a fishing day. I went to the Wenning to celebrate my success, hoping to make perfection of a day already close to it by catching a brown trout or two. In those days I was easily satisfied; in those days just one good trout could make the whole day glorious.

I cannot recall all the details of that day more than forty years ago. I remember sunshine and a soft breeze. I remember swallows in the sky and wagtails bobbing on the stones. I know that the river was falling back from spate and beginning to shine with the deep amber glow that in later years would tell me to fish wet flies upstream; but on that late August day more than forty years ago I still thought of myself as a dry fly purist; I had learned my fishing mostly from books and it was from these that I had absorbed this ridiculous pose, looking askance at men who fished flies designed to sink and filled their creels. It was nonsense and I would soon learn better ways but, on that day late in August when the morning post brought good news and I took my happiness to the Wenning, hoping to turn it into something even happier, I was still a disciple of Halford, still a clumsy and ignorant exponent of the dry fly. In those days I was much better at Latin and Greek than at catching trout.

Much of that late August day is lost to me, but I know that I fished my way right to the first pool of the river and then way up Clapham Beck, much further than I had ever been before. I cannot remember what fly I was fishing; whatever it was, I do remember that it had caught me a few fish, small and mostly parr, and that they had all gone back; most of all I remember that the afternoon was warm and that my thoughts were just as soft and comfortable as the encompassing air, for the young man on the edge of the water was, to his own mind's eye, a scholar as well as a fisherman, a man of letters as much as a man of the riverbank, and the life that stretched ahead of him was a life full of Horace and Homer and Virgil, and

141

full of days by running water and full of trout. It was a wonderful prospect and it was a delight, anyway, to be exploring water that I had never fished before, miniature water that brought a new feature every second or third footfall.

Some time late in the afternoon the blue wings came; they came drifting thickly down the tiny pools, clustering on every corner and trapped in untidy lines against each trailing willow branch. They came thickly down the water and the air all round me was full of their fluttering. In those days I always greeted the appearance of blue wings with special pleasure, partly because I had read so much about them in chalkstream literature, which made them seem insects with distinctly aristocratic connections, but also because, with their three tails, they were among the few flies that I could identify with real confidence. They made me feel an expert.

It was a big hatch and the trout rose greedily. I caught nothing of any note, but I persuaded myself that two of my fish were at least nine inches long and so big enough to kill (which they may well have been). I caught nothing remarkable, although a brace of trout in my bag, even if they were barely takeable, was in those days itself an achievement. I had caught nothing to live brightly in the memory, although I was very happy with my brace of small trout; but then, under a straggling willow that dipped its branches in the water on a sharp corner, I saw a rise and my fly fell right and I turned my wrist and knew at once that I had hooked a monster.

Perhaps he was a brooding cannibal, tempted from his dark lair by the untypical profusion of fly. I still believe that, for the Wenning and its becks, he was a very big fish; I think that he weighed at least two pounds, which was much heavier than any trout that I had ever hooked before and a whole pound heavier than any that I had both hooked and killed. He was a huge trout and he was on for perhaps thirty seconds, but it was beyond my skill to manage him and he smashed my nylon with savage contempt, leaving me standing there on the edge of the water, standing there shaking with excitement and struggling to cope with the anguished frustration of loss.

Three or four times I pulled slack line through the rod rings, hoping against hope that my trout had not really gone, hoping that, if only I pulled long enough, I should feel his angry presence again as my rod sprang back to life. But there was nothing: nothing but a dangling length of limp and hookless nylon. And suddenly all the pleasure of a soft afternoon in August had dissolved onto the air, taking with it all my pride in those high examination grades. I was no longer a scholar-fisherman; I was only a defeated young angler, oppressed by the misery of his failure and feeling, for all his twenty summers, on the edge of tears.

For a novice fisher, losing a big trout is a bitter and wounding experience; it leaves scars. The sudden collapse of tension, the giddy descent from wild delight to that sudden and aching sense of separation, all this is too much to come to terms within a few hours or even in the course of a few days. Losing a big trout is often a difficult experience for fishers of many years; for an unseasoned fisher it is almost more than he can bear. It is, I imagine, rather like falling off a mountain or being jilted in love. Whatever it is like, it hurts abominably. For weeks I was troubled by the grim memory of my brief contact with the monster of Clapham Beck. Throughout September, if the water was flowing full, I fished quickly up the Wenning and went in search of him. But, even though the blue wings came thickly again a time or two, I saw nothing rising beneath his willow bush and I never again caught a trout longer than nine or ten inches from his pool on the corner or from any of the little pools that belonged to his winding beck.

With the passing of my undergraduate days I fished the Wenning less often; I had discovered another river where the trout were so much more plentiful that a day spent in the shadow of Ingleborough seemed almost a wasted fishing day. I had found the Wharfe at Kilnsey and, within a year or two, I had joined the Kilnsey Angling Club, abandoning the little Wenning altogether - except for one visit to her which came at the end, not of a fishing day but of a long day in the hills. It was a visit without a fishing rod, it was unaccompanied by any predatory thoughts and it was intended as a sort of sentimental homage to times past. It confounded my expectations by turning into a painful and very bitter reunion, for I found, as I wandered up the fields in search of warm memories, that I was not walking along the river that I had once fished; I was not looking at a proper river at all, with those eccentric features that flowing water always creates when left to express itself in its own way. Instead of this I was looking at a flat channel of water creeping along in the shadow of steep and regularly shelving banks. I was looking at a canal; I was looking at a ditch; I was looking at the latest achievement of the men of the River Board and I was sickened by what I saw.

It was, of course, the result of a completely unnecessary flood-prevention scheme and it poisoned my memories of the little river, so that for years I tried not to think of her and even tried to forget my meeting with the monster of Clapham Beck. I swore that I should never again fish the Wenning or bring myself the pain of walking along her banks.

———◆———

It was at least twenty years later when, at the start of another season, a friend told me that, although the Wenning was not the river she had once been, she was at least half mended and was well worth fishing again. Within a week I had bought a ticket for my old stretch of the river and spent a spring day there. There was a big hatch of olives and I came home with three or four trout and with the feeling that I had re-established a precious friendship. Yes, the little river was scarred and would never be as she had once been, but there was more of the old river left than my eyes had told me on the day of that bitter re-acquaintance twenty years ago.

My return to the Wenning was a great joy to me, although it was not without its portion of pain. On the first day of my return I had left Clapham Beck unfished because the hatch had already failed by the time I reached the top of the river. But I was back on the Wenning the next day and this time I was determined to fish the beck and find the corner where the monster had broken me. I went in search of his corner and was dismayed to find that it was no longer there.

I had for some reason assumed that the tributary becks had remained unmolested, but now I found that Clapham Beck had been even more cruelly treated than the river. It had been straightened and confined and they seemed somehow to have diminished its flow; it was clear to me at least that Clapham Beck was now a much smaller watercourse than the winding stream I had once fished with such delight. And there were places where I could walk along the wandering line of the old beck, treading on a dry confusion of boulders and pebbles and tufts of grass. There were sickly willows leaning over rocky hollows that had once been pools; there were great slabs of concrete trapping a sad trickle of water between hard and unresponsive banks.

I found the stump of an old willow on what might once have been a corner with a pool in its shadow. This could be the place, I told myself, where the monster of Clapham Beck had broken me all those years ago. I had come to the beck, hoping to find his corner and feel the presence of his ghost hovering over the water. It was planned as part of my repossession of the Wenning and its becks and now it could not happen because there was no water, no pool, no corner and no sense of a lingering presence from a now distant summer. I had intended, as my mind surrendered to images from the past, to tell the monster of Clapham Beck that all was forgiven; I intended, in fact, to thank him for his brief appearance in my life, for over the years I had come to realise that his sudden departure from it, although it had been very painful at the time, had helped me to realise how catching trout was a central part of my happiness, inspiring me with the determination to catch trout even bigger than the monster that I had lost. Time and again the taming and capture of a big fish, and the joy that comes with it, has turned my mind to the emptiness that overwhelmed me when the monster of Clapham Beck broke my line, and whenever this has happened I have recognised how, without that emptiness, there could not be this present joy.

On that afternoon by Clapham Beck, as I stood where there might once have been a pool and a corner and a trailing willow, I could not do what I had intended because I could not recapture the past. The sense of loss was too great and so I was unable finally to make my peace with the monster of Clapham Beck.

I have now found the past again by writing about it; I have found too that at last I can say hail and farewell to the trout that has haunted me for more than forty years. Once again I acknowledge that he has, after all, been a kind and powerful presence in my life, and so, in taking my leave of him, I pray that, wherever he lies, earth or water may press lightly upon his bones.

Also published by Merlin Unwin Books

The Fisherman's Bedside Book
BB £18.95

Once a Flyfisher
Laurence Catlow £17.99

Moonlighting: tales and misadventures of a working life with eels
Michael Brown £15.99

The Secret Carp
Chris Yates £17.99

Flycasting Skills John Symonds £9.99

Trout from a Boat Dennis Moss £16

The Pocket Guide to Matching the Hatch
Peter Lapsley and Cyril Bennett £7.99

The Pocket Guide to Fishing Knots
Step-by-Step Coarse, Sea and Game Knots
Peter Owen £5.99

The Beginner's Guide to Flytying
Chris Mann and Terry Griffiths £9.99

The Complete Illustrated Directory of Salmon Flies
Chris Mann £20

Trout in Dirty Places
Theo Pike £20

Canal Fishing
Dominic Garnett £20

Flyfishing for Coarse Fish
Dominic Garnett £20

Fishing with Harry
Tony Baws £15.99

How to Flyfish
John Symonds £9.99

Fishing with Emma
David Overland £9.99

Flies of Ireland
Peter O'Reilly £20